Psychotherapy and the Terrorized Patient

Psychotherapy and the Terrorized Patient

E. Mark Stern, Editor
Iona College, New Rochelle, New York

The Haworth Press
New York

Psychotherapy and the Terrorized Patient has also been published as *The Psychotherapy Patient,* Volume 1, Number 4, Summer 1985.

© 1985 by The Haworth Press, Inc. All rights reserved. No part of this work may be reproduced or utilized in any form or by any means, electronic or mechanical, including photocopying, microfilm and recording, or by any information storage and retrieval system without permission in writing from the publisher. Printed in the United States of America.

The Haworth Press, Inc., 28 East 22 Street, New York, NY 10010

Library of Congress Cataloging in Publication Data
Main entry under title:

Psychotherapy and the terrorized patient.

"Has also been published as the Psychotherapy patient,
Volume 1, No. 4, Summer 1985"—T.p. verso.
Includes bibliographies.
1. Terror. 2. Psychotherapy. I. Stern, E. Mark, 1929- .
RC535.P79 1985   616.85'206   85-8468
ISBN 0-86656-442-X

Psychotherapy and the Terrorized Patient

The Psychotherapy Patient
Volume 1, Number 4

CONTENTS

Introduction   **1**

Keeping Faith with the Terrorized Patient: A Dialogue   **3**
Virginia Fraser Stern
E. Mark Stern

Two Terrorized Patients: Some Wartime Recollections   **11**
Martin Grotjahn

Terrorized Voices   12

Terror and Its Treatment   **13**
John H. Gagnon

**The Headless Toy Soldiers: The Terrorization of a Patient
by Unsoothing Introjects**   **27**
Juana Culhane

Power and Terror of Change   **33**
Lawrence Tirnauer

Parameters of Power   33
Cultural Imperatives   34
Essentials of Power   34
The Power of Terror   34
The Pursuit of Power   35
Power and Abuse   35
Helplessness and Power   36
Projection and Helplessness   37
Combined Power and Helplessness   38

The Psychotherapy Patient and the Initial Session: What to Do with the Emotional State   **39**
    Alvin R. Mahrer
    Henry P. Edwards
    Gary M. Durak
    Irit Sterner

  Method   41
  Results and Discussion   43

Primitive Agonies   **49**
    Elizabeth M. Ellis

Healing the Terrorized Patient as a Model for Healing a Terrorized World   **61**
    Kenneth Wapnick

  Introduction   61
  The World of Terror   62
  The Psychology of Terror   65
  Psychotherapy as the End of Terror   68
  The Role of the Holy Spirit   71

The Terrorized Patient as Brutalized Person   **75**
    James E. Dublin

Integrating the Splits in Crime Victims' Self Images: Toward the Reparation of the Damaged Self   **87**
    Sharon Hymer

  Splitting   88
  The Three Primary Levels   89
  Splits in Self-Image: Two Illustrations   92
  Conclusion   96

I Was an Incest Victim   **99**
    Anonymous

Incest 1964: Confusion and Terror 1984   **105**
    Barbara Jo Brothers

Entitlement: A Meditation for the Psychotherapy Patient (To be read aloud to oneself)   **111**
Joseph C. Zinker

Introduction	111
I. The World and My Beloved	111
II. Nature	112
III. People	112
IV. Work	113
V. Relatives	114
VI. On Being a Victim	115

EDITOR

E. MARK STERN, Ed.D., A.B.P.P., *Iona College, New Rochelle, NY; Private practice, New York, NY*

HONORARY EDITOR

MARIE COLEMAN NELSON, *Amani Counselling Centre, Nairobi, Kenya*

ASSOCIATE EDITOR

JEROME TRAVERS, Ph.D., *Private practice, Summit, NJ*

MANAGING EDITOR

GENEVIEVE IZINICKI, M.S.W., A.C.S.W., *Private practice, New York, NY*

EDITORIAL BOARD

BARBARA ANN BECHER, Ph.D., I.A.P.C.P., *Private practice, Jamaica, NY; Catholic Charities, Mineola, NY*
ARNOLD BERNSTEIN, Ph.D., *Private practice; Center for Modern Psychoanalytic Studies, New York, NY*
ROBERT BURNS, Ph.D., *Iona College, New Rochelle, NY; Private practice, New York, NY*
RUDOLPH D. CALABRESE, M.S.W., *Private practice, Melville, NY*
JUSTIN CAREY, Ph.D., *St. John's University, Jamaica, NY*
ALBERT ELLIS, Ph.D., *Institute for Rational Emotive Therapy, New York, NY*
ROBERT GOULDING, M.D., *Western Institute for Group and Family Therapy, Watsonville, CA*
MARC HANDELMAN, Ph.D., *Private practice, New York, NY; Brooklyn Community Counseling Center, Brooklyn, NY*
JAMES LAY, Ph.D., *New York Institute for Gestalt Therapy, New York, NY*
EVELYN LIPKIN, M.S.W., *George Williams College, Downer's Grove, IL*
JAMES LLOYD, Ph.D., *Iona College, New Rochelle, NY*
KAREN MACHOVER, M.A., *Private practice, New York, NY*
ALVIN MAHRER, Ph.D., *University of Ottawa, Ottawa, Canada*
JOSEPH MARTORANO, M.D., *Premenstrual Tension Medical Group, New York, NY*
PATRICK SEAN MOFFETT, Ph.D., *Iona College, New Rochelle, NY*
SAMUEL NATALE, D. Phil., *Private practice, Teaneck, NJ; University of Bridgeport, Bridgeport, CT*
LAURA PERLS, D.Sc., *New York Institute for Gestalt Therapy, New York, NY*
VIRGINIA SATIR, M.S.W., *Anterra, Inc., Palo Alto, CA*
BERTRAM SCHAFFNER, M.D., *Private practice; William Alanson White Institute, New York, NY*
WILLIAM VICIC, M.D., *St. Vincent's Hospital Center, New York, NY*
KENNETH WAPNICK, Ph.D., *Foundation for a Course in Miracles, Crompond, NY*
BARRY WEPMAN, Ph.D., *Private practice, Florham Park, NJ*
ERIKA WICK, Ph.D., *St. John's University, Jamaica, NY*

Psychotherapy and the Terrorized Patient

Introduction

Under the firm crust of the planet dwell powerful forces of nature, which, as soon as some accident affords them free play, must necessarily destroy the crust with everything living upon it, as had already taken place at least three times upon our planet, and will probably take place oftener still. The earthquake of Lisbon, the earthquake of Haiti, the destruction of Pompeii, are only small hints of what is possible. Arthur Schopenhauer

As with the philosopher, those faced with fears of imminent peril see optimism as the bitter mockery of human woes. These words written by Arthur Schopenhauer express the pangs of uncertainty and dread experienced unceasingly by a terrorized segment of the population. Those branded with terror who eventually seek the services of contemporary psychotherapists often appear to share many of the developmental dynamics common to those others who scale the razor's edge separating sanity from its more troubled counterparts. Yet for them the variations of dread are the metaphors for impending universal catastrophe. Thoroughly awestruck by the potential for earthquakes, tidal waves, and all-consuming fires, the names of terrorized patients are rarely seen on the mastheads of alliances protesting the production of nuclear weapons. And though hyperaware of personal peril, they shun the challenges of escalating environmental hazards or appeals for greater product safety. Contaminated by overwhelming fears, terrorized patients feel compelled to choke off most tracings of contentment and gratification. As if in hiding, such patients avoid moving into the counterflow of reassurance.

Sometimes labeled agoraphobic, paranoid, eccentric, or just contrary, terrorized patients claim to see the tracings of a grim reality. To them, earth is porous with the potential for disaster, with myths of disaster, and the perils of mortality. Yet it must be said in their favor that each moment of fear links itself to the torments of being fully alive.

To the terrorized, fear and awe-filled horror are spurs to a specialized version of reality. Held spellbound by torturesome fears, such individuals seek psychotherapy as an acceptable incantation to the scathing horrors of existence. For them life runs a course rife with peril and agitation. Being faced with such patients, it behooves the psychotherapist to barter a portion of such terror for reason. Invariably frustrated in this task, it then falls upon a therapist's shoulders to help savor whatever life forces remain encased within the territories of terror. Central to this commission is

© 1985 by The Haworth Press, Inc. All rights reserved.

a willingness to travel that extra mile to the edge of the feared abyss. An additional requirement is the ability to resist all temptations to force-feed optimism and reassurance. To do so would diminish appropriate therapeutic inventiveness and creativity.

Assembled in this volume is a wellspring of clinical vantage points. Each contribution maintains its own format and proposed interventions. For the reader this means a less than certain voyage into what is and is not sure about the management of the terrified personality. As in all volumes of this open-ended series, this collection seeks to be an open-ended attempt at creating significant groundwork for continuing inquiry.

E. Mark Stern
Editor

Keeping Faith with the Terrorized Patient: A Dialogue

Virginia Fraser Stern
E. Mark Stern

E. Mark Stern: A definition of terms: Terror is not necessarily synonymous with anxiety. Moreover, when referring to terrorized individuals, it is best that they not be confused with patients who simply anticipate the worst because of avoidable inefficiencies in given responsibilities. Terror is distinct. It is suggestive of living close to the abyss—an abyss characterized by primal chaos. Included are people who daily fear nuclear holocaust yet are fearful of getting involved in work aimed at ameliorating such threats. These are people who live in the wake of a dubious future with little notion of how to galvanize the necessary resources to cope with the deadly prospects of such a future.

Virginia Fraser Stern: I was thinking of a terrorized patient of mine who anticipates an involuntary hurtling toward the abyss despite his brave attempts at staying alive. It's as if terror has become meaning, and destruction a fascination. His early childhood was characterized by being subject to intimidating threats. This was coupled with unceasing attempts at being a "good boy" though he never actually felt that he'd achieved that goal. There could be no emotional payoff because nothing he ever did was "good enough." His father was a very strong military type and his mother an angry alcoholic. There could be no way of pleasing either of them.

EMS: I hear you implying that terrorized patients are disconnected because the worst has, in fact, already happened—something like anticipating a sonic boom in the wake of a combat jet. In my experience such people are usually loners. They lack the essential ability to establish

---

Virginia Fraser Stern, MS from Columbia University in 1975, is a Certified Social Worker in the private practice of individual, couple, and group psychotherapy. 215 East Eleventh Street, New York, NY 10003.

E. Mark Stern, EdD, completed his clinical studies at Columbia University (1955) and at the Institute of the National Psychological Association for Psychoanalysis. Besides his private practice in psychotherapy and psychoanalysis, Dr. Stern is Professor in the Graduate Division of Pastoral Counseling, Iona College, New Rochelle, New York, and is on the faculty of the American Institute for Psychotherapy and Psychoanalysis in New York City. Dr. Stern is a Diplomate in Clinical Psychology of the American Board of Professional Psychology. 215 East Eleventh Street, New York, NY 10003.

© 1985 by The Haworth Press, Inc. All rights reserved.

relationships except on the grounds of setting up the other person as a source of reassurance. This ultimately transforms itself into an angry demand that the other person always be understanding.

VFS: One thing is clear. We are talking about people who are caught up in the developmental world of an abandoned 2-year-old. As emotional 2-year-olds, they may have enough consciousness to want to go out to do things for themselves, yet because of a lack of resources they appear to be constantly looking for someone "greater" or more sure-footed than themselves to supply the necessary resources. The task is to turn developmental devastation into something productive.

EMS: Terrorized people appear to walk around with their fragile selves up front. They seem to not have developed a sense of what goes beyond a functioning self. For me, that which is outside the limitations of self is soul or animating principle—though this is not precisely what is implied in a religious sense. I think rather of inclusion in a network in life. If this vital spirit is not advanced, then the self, by force of circumstance, becomes fragile and terrified. Outside this network of life, terrorized people fail to connect with a significant other. Consequently, terrified individuals often sport fantasies of being big hoaxes—of being the only alive person on earth. This terror of being alone is part of a young child's development. But we've come to expect a resolution as the years go on. If, however, one feels cut off, then terror and panic can be expected to continue. Life itself becomes the haunted trick.

VFS: I think that's true. The idea of life being a setup or a trick plays a fairly large role in all-encompassing terror. Terror becomes the life-style rather than an occasional episode. If all of life is tied up in such terror then there's an obvious fear of letting go of it.

EMS: Like a child who fears sleep—who'd rather the distrust of the darkness than the comfort of letting go.

VFS: Recall the patient I referred to when we began. Although terrorized, he continues to have an image of himself as potentially effective—of connecting more of himself to life. He's really quite bright and sensitive, yet he defeats himself at every turn. Job interviews rarely work out because of his defensive terror. He appears unable to afford to connect himself to what he considers someone else's expectations. Psychodynamically, he's not been able to work his way out of the devastation he felt at his parents' hands. What has resulted is his avoidance of any kind of authority figures inasmuch as even the best of bosses is seen in the role of the abusive parent. Typically, my patient's parents were destructive teasers, with expectations that could never be met.

EMS: I gather that your patient sees himself as the runt of the litter, living as he does in an overpowering and terrifying transference.

VFS: He made a serious attempt at having a meaningful relationship with his sister—the one person who seemed significantly appreciated by others in the family. Unfortunately, he had a single incestuous experience with her. Shortly thereafter she killed herself. What followed became the representation of the whole world for him. His one attempt at trying to love was not only twisted up in its inappropriate circumstance but now had become absolutely frightening. He could not be sure that he didn't cause her suicide, even though his sister had been a serious substance abuser and had apparently killed herself as a result of a narcotic overdose. My patient connected it all together and came out feeling that it had all been his fault.

EMS: Terrorized patients' paranoid defenses act as accommodations to their terror. Paranoia becomes the life-style. The other person's vulnerability becomes justification of their own terror. It's certainly not uncommon to hear terrorized patients allude to another person's frightening misfortunes. It seems on the surface that it's happened to them. But with a difference. They feel condemned to waiting in horror for the moment when it is expected to happen to them. It's an introduction to what they fear most—punishment, abandonment, and finally, the abyss. The terrorized patient has no faith in being emotionally redeemed from the fates. They tend to seek out a lot of therapy or, in its place, self-help tracks of one sort or another. Yet it's not simply hopelessness in the face of the abyss. They simply do not trust that anybody has the skills to match up to their terrors.

VFS: There's another side still. As in all psychological ways of being, two thrusts go on. One, the person wants not to be terrorized; and two, there is the attraction, and sometimes the addiction, to the terror. It's as if nothing else can feel quite as real. There was recently a big county fair near our country home. Recall the ''scary'' rides and the kids going on them again and again—obviously fascinated by the terror the rides evoked. The terror serves as proof of one's ability to survive the demons, though to adults it's an obvious hype, both stimulating and fascinating. The therapeutic task with terror involves getting to the excitement but beyond the terror, thereby connecting the patient to the larger world.

Perhaps the inverse excitement of terror gives a person a way out of being too much part of the mainstream. The patient I have cited may say that he'd like a prestigious job on Wall Street. Yet, despite such stated ambitions, I get the feeling that he wants to preserve his ''outsider'' status, because in a strange way it makes him feel more alive.

EMS: So what you're saying is that terrorized patients often come across as eternal aliens. Yet being on the outside does not necessarily exclude them from looking for skills which make it possible to adapt to a social mainstream.

VFS: As aliens, perhaps it makes sense to help them become better at learning to live with terror. My patient, while essentially remaining a loner, begins to find ways and resources within himself of relating to the world. Now I certainly don't think he has to be doomed to terror. I would not want to take his terror away any more than I would his excitement. If I tried to administer relief, chances are he'd become overly suspicious and draw back into a private craziness. Rather than simply relieve his terror, I find it more fruitful to correlate whatever active dread he feels with the world in which he lives.

EMS: Managing therapy with terrorized patients requires helping them gain something of the sophistication of the outsider. After all, the terrorized person feels that he or she knows something that the rest of us are unfamiliar with. I somehow relate the sane side of terror to the prophetic insights of a biblical Jeremiah. Jeremiah is the archetype of the outsider who says in substance, "Behold the perils of existence." Living on the pessimistic side of being requires grounding in the healthy terrors of a life. Free-floating anxiety is often the escape route from authentic terror.

VFS: The more seriously one takes the terror the more comfort the patient gets. However, the more the psychotherapist attempts to solve the anxiety by reassuring the patient, the less insight seems to follow. It may be a pretty simple formula, but it does prove out.

EMS: That their terror has worth?

VFS: Well, we're all terrified.

EMS: And beyond terror, such patients are anxious. Characteristically this anxiety is based on feelings of separation and isolation. The key is always in how one connects terror to the larger world.

VFS: The clinical rule is to watch your timing in bringing this to the fore. It took me a good year and a half with my patient before there was enough relationship for me to say, "Yes, your terror is really not different from my own, but you seem to feel it more." If I had started making connections earlier in our work, he would have bolted. Since the terror may have seemed to be his only sense of power, it was also his aliveness and vitality. Everything else may pale in the face of such intensity. Terror does, in some way, correlate with what some people refer to as peak experiences. Both connect to a sensation of aliveness. Terror is not the same as being frightened.

EMS: Something like, "I am terrorized, therefore I am."

VFS: Very much so. The depressed person is afraid to give up depression. Likewise, terrorized paranoia is self-perpetuating. It all represents a fear of ridding oneself of behaviors attached to patterns of survival.

EMS: Survival on the edge of a whirlpool! One thing I have found helpful with some terrorized people has been to foster some means of their facing their most terrifying fears within the therapeutic situation. I try to heighten the intensity of what they're most frightened of. For example, the possibility of losing a job. I've gotten to the point of seeing how the enactment of such a fear foments the undoing of a sense of connection with the world—leaving them fearful of existing in a depersonalized abyss. Such ego-centered terror becomes one basis for feelings of imminent world disaster. It's hard to approach such gross terror. To a patient fearful that the bomb would fall any minute, I once said, "Let's take it 5 minutes beyond that. See yourself dead right now. Try to honor that experience." To extend such terror into its most fantastical dire consequence permits the patient a right to his or her reality. Once the terror and its consequences are located, it may be helpful to work with biofeedback. Biofeedback and other meditative approaches permit an extension into and beyond the most horrifying terror. Because such techniques focus on letting go, these practices should only be instituted within controlled circumstances. Leading a patient to that sense of an abyss can lead to several levels of approaching freedom. As I see it, the initial level conforms to Kübler-Ross' (1969) stages in her work with dying patients. Kübler-Ross notes first "denial and isolation" where I have observed *dissociation and personal depreciation.* Kübler-Ross foresees "anger" as a second stage, where I see *exacerbation of terror.* And skipping over her third stage of "bargaining" to a fourth stage, "depression," my sense of the terrorized patient's journey to the abyss goes now to a *resigned dread.* And finally, Kübler-Ross' fourth stage, "acceptance," becomes the common ground of realizing that the fates do not plunder but can, in fact, be kind. Techniques involving imagery and mild trance states can help punctuate the journey from a disassociated inner depreciation in the face of threat to what amounts to a quiet acceptance.

Questions about the feasibility of medication often arise. In my opinion medication is rarely helpful with truly terrorized patients. Physicians sometimes mistake terror for anxiety, and thus prescribe phenothiazenes which have the disadvantage of making some terrorized patients feel they're losing their bearings. It's as if they don't know what to do with their chemically induced deadness.

VFS: I think any of us in the healing professions want to make people feel better. One of the hardest things I've had to learn as a therapist over the past 10 years is to resist that impulse. Over the years I've found that what's truly helpful is to not try to ameliorate the necessary discomfort, but instead to help terrorized patients be more connected to whatever they feel. Mind you, that can be very painful for me at times—although as the years go on I get a little better at it. It's no easy matter to sit with somebody week after week and help them simply become more connected to the discomfort, the pain, and the terror that they're feeling. It certainly touches discordant notes in me, resulting in the tendency to say, "Gee, I want to make you feel better. How can I help you feel better?" Anybody in a position to write a prescription may want to induce tranquility. It may be fortunate that a whole host of therapists are not able to prescribe. They don't have the "quick cure" to rely on. All in all, I agree with you that ultimately drugs don't help. The patient I've been adverting to has been taking some medication since a recent hospitalization. He has gotten used to it, and it may be of some slight assistance in controlling his impulsive behavior. But he went through a terribly frightening period just after he began the medication. It made him feel more deadened and, as you say, increased his sense of terror rather than decreasing it. But as a way of regulating impulsive behavior, medication helped protect my patient from angry lashing-out at others.

EMS: You mean that his compulsive acting out had something to do with——

VFS: Fights, arguments, baiting, being paranoid. The clerk at the supermarket or some guy walking along the street might accidentally knock into him and he was convinced that this person meant him harm. As a result, he would immediately bristle and want to start a fight. Sometimes he'd bait and bait and bait until an angry confrontation would ensue.

EMS: I wonder if what has been labeled post-traumatic stress is not in fact a form of terror. As the other side of feeling terror, one may, like your patient, inflict terror. I tend to see this as a result of the anticipatory anxiety related to having experienced trauma. I hesitate using the term anticipatory anxiety because I doubt that one can anticipate more than a narrow range of hurts. Terror has a crescendo all its own which builds up to a greater and greater pitch and finally through to reach a climactic moment. Yet it's been my experience that highly terrorized patients are rarely very sexual, either in their acting out or in their daily social intercourse.

VFS: I think they're not very sexual. Good sexuality implies an orgiastic release. When a terrorized patient reaches orgasm he or she may experience an initial sense of relief but afterwards, having looked back at "letting go," may become even more frightened of being open to victimization, and the resulting meaninglessness and powerlessness.

EMS: So you're saying that even their orgasms, which in principle then promised relief, become for them the stuff of anticipatory terror. They therefore avoid orgasm or any other variety of climactic experience.

VFS: I'm saying they have a paradoxical way of talking about their life. On the one hand, the terrorized patient is saying, "I want relief." Yet, on the other hand, such patients may not really want what they cry out for. Terror is the only thing that's real to them. As a result they don't in fact get more terrorized or less terrorized, just more frightened. The acting out becomes an attempt at dissipating feelings of powerlessness. In the face of all this, what then should be the psychotherapist's role? The sentiments might go something like this: "Ah, yes, I hear your terror. . . . I'm trying to understand it. . . . I'll try to accompany you on your journey. . . . Let's just see where we go. . . . Be sure that I will be here." In my view, it's the *constancy* of the therapist that's basic. Certainly not 24-hour-a-day availability—not at all. To my mind it's the constancy of caring—of being responsible and reliable so that the relationship itself begins to give the terrorized person a little bit of a fingerhold on life.

EMS: Once again, I'm glad you didn't say relief because that would be what the terrorized person is unable to cope with. I sense that you're talking about "a fingerhold on life" as a means of adaptation. Who is to say what an individual's mode of existence ought to be? All we know is what are charged to do is to be able to facilitate a person's sense of what he or she feels is most appropriate.

VFS: That's right. There are a multitude of ways and shades of being. There are people in the middle, more who are on the outside. And ultimately who knows what the outside is anyway? There are many middles—but maybe even more outsides. Together you and I are raising three children. I probably know them more than I know anyone else in life. I look at all three of them and I'm amazed at how different each one of them is, and how little I have to do with any of it.

EMS: It's been said by a psychotherapist friend of mine, Dr. Vincent O'Connell, that good therapy is knowing how and when to interrupt. As with raising a child, working with the terrorized patient is knowing when *not* to interrupt.

VFS: It's a matter of artful timing, but more important, it's a matrix of caring—a project of being available to another person. I sometimes say, "You may feel cut off. But you're really not alone. I'm around." Beyond timing, it's a matter of constancy. Even so, you can't "do it" for somebody.

EMS: Doesn't this require a particular kind of therapist? Something unique with the therapist? For example, do terrorized therapists work well with terrorized patients? Or would the terror of the patient correspond *too much* with the terror of the therapist? I think there are therapists who, because of their own terror, are familiar with the potential and the possibility in that terror.

VFS: Like anything else, I think the distinction is the quality of insight and control the therapist has. Working with a terrorized person is frequently not very active work if one has one's bearings. The therapist must be willing and able to stand back while being alert. The terrorized patient will just pull away if the therapist is too active.

EMS: The terrorized patient is hardly capable of providing the therapist with the professional nourishment he or she may require. These patients rarely express any positive acknowledgments. Nevertheless, if one is willing to work with them, the therapist must remain constant and available. But this too has its own rewards. Terror closes off as it opens up the possibility of a valid pessimistic world view. Pessimism, while not at all popular or inviting, keeps company with some notions of where the world is going. Terrorized patients provide an opportunity to see this sense of life develop into maladaptive behavior. The question is how close to the abyss can a person truly stand without regressing to fury and destructiveness. Surely the psychotherapist can be of help in providing enough mature expectations to help tip the balance of the scale in favor of growth.

REFERENCE

Kübler-Ross, E. (1969). *On death and dying.* New York: MacMillan.

Two Terrorized Patients:
Some Wartime Recollections

Martin Grotjahn

When working as a psychiatrist in the Medical Corps of the United States Army, I had to attend to a small, haggard-looking man, ill-nourished, dehydrated, badly colored skin, run-down, and exhausted. His papers showed that he was an officer, otherwise I knew nothing. He himself could not talk, was in a deep catatonic stupor, occasionally looking around with terror-stricken eyes. Even in pentothal narcosis he could not be reached, but remained mute.

Red Cross, social workers, comrades, chaplain, and superior officers told enough to piece together the story: The officer had been a captain before the war and hired himself out to rich people. He knew the South Sea Islands, their Bays and beaches, their coral reefs and free waters, fishing grounds, and sea routes like nobody else.

During the "island hopping" he turned out to be of great value to the invading forces. He had great courage, was promoted with several battlefield promotions, and was decorated. He never complained; he was always there, ready to go into action again; and so he participated in almost every invasion.

One day he was lying in a mosquito- and malaria-infected swamp, bored and exhausted, threatened by unseen enemies and feeling heavily the responsibility for his men. He had been in many such situations and it had almost become his way of life.

Then mail arrived. He was most astonished that there was a big letter for him—he who rarely, if ever, received mail, since he lived alone and seemed to have no family. The letter informed him in legal lingo that one of his rich former employers left him an enormous fortune in gratitude and grateful recollection of some delightful adventures in the utopian peace of the South Sea Islands.

On that afternoon he broke down. It seems as if he had been perfectly willing to risk his life in combat as long as he was poor and—in a way—

Martin Grotjahn studied medicine in Berlin, Germany, and has been a psychiatrist since 1929 and a psychoanalyst since 1936 when he came to the United States. Dr. Grotjahn is Professor Emeritus of Psychiatry at the University of Southern California and Training Analyst Emeritus at the Southern California Institute for Psychoanalysis.

© 1985 by The Haworth Press, Inc. All rights reserved.

11

had little to lose. But now he was a man of substance, of wealth, and he could not risk an existence which seemed to promise a true paradise.

I do not know what happened to this man. It was my impression that he had served enough for his country and probably would never again be able to work in the field. I wrote his retirement papers and know that he was eventually sent home. From general experience I would guess that he recovered in due time to enjoy a new life.

TERRORIZED VOICES

Once a gigantic man was sent to me because he was found to hallucinate quietly and continually. His superiors were worried whether he could stand a ceremonial decoration planned for him on the following day.

He told me in his quiet way that he had been hospitalized often and altogether had spent several years in mental hospitals in the years before the war. At the induction board examination somebody asked him whether he heard voices? And he had answered quietly and truthfully with "Yes." The officers in charge laughed aloud and passed him as well qualified because of his wonderful sense of humor. In his schizophrenic detachment he did well in training and was soon sent to the front. The constant hearing of voices bothered him somewhat but seemed to have interfered with his duties little or not at all. He told nobody about it and did his duty almost mechanically, obediently, and to everybody's satisfaction.

He was caught in a retreat with everybody leaving him, he being left alone with his machine gun in his trench. He never had much contact with his comrades and so he was not truly aware of what was happening. He did his duty like always and this meant holding an entire onrushing horde of the enemy at bay. The voices, always so sarcastic to him, declared him finally as being caught "behind the 8-ball" and stated coolly, "This gets too hot for us; we quit." Then he did not hear them for a while.

It was many hours before his comrades could return, and they found him at his post. His heroic action was recognized and he was recommended for a promotion and decoration with a citation and military ceremonies. The evening before the great event was to take place the voices returned and now at closer inspection he seemed to behave peculiarly to his comrades and superior officers. He was finally sent for psychiatric observation.

He was diagnosed as a chronic schizophrenic who should be transferred to a veteran's hospital. There he was, left to his own adaptative behavior, defective as it may have appeared to others. It was also recommended that he should receive his decoration, but that he should be discharged. There should be no military ceremonies. Since the Army felt uneasy about the situation, this seemed to be the right way out for everybody and for once the psychiatric recommendations were followed.

Terror and Its Treatment

John H. Gagnon

ABSTRACT. For 12 years the author has worked with the disordered lives of many human beings. Both in institutional settings as well as in his private practice, the author has seen individuals meet their own "monsters" and face the parts of themselves with which they found their own terrors, their own "hells on earth." John himself had to face feeling intense terror. He used the experience of terror in himself as an empathic tool to help others. In this article the author recounts his own journey into the subject of terror, tells a few "tales of terror" and ends with some theoretical suggestions about the nature of "terror" and its treatment.

As I sit in front of the gray-cased word processor in the living room of our tiny cabin I look out the windows, hear the chirping of small birds beneath the sill, and watch the red and golden colors wash from the sky over Rainbow Lake. I am beginning to write this paper for E. Mark Stern's new journal about patients. I find my thoughts drifting away from the approaching darkness of this April day to another "darkness" with which I am all too familiar. Mark has asked me to write about the "terrorized patient" and even the word "terror" seems, somehow, much more appropriate than the other synonyms which I might have chosen: anxious, fearful, worried. No mere work like "anxiety" can so correctly capture the dread, the intensity of foreboding, the very horror of living which I have seen in so many of my therapy patients and have even experienced in myself both within and outside of the therapeutic process in the last 12 years. And it is about this phenomenon of *terror* which I intend to write.

Most of the patients in the Day Treatment Program of Danbury Hospital (approximately 25/day) were diagnosed as being schizophrenic based on the criteria that they were often hallucinating, delusional, autistic, and the like (Freedman & Kaplan, 1967). When we received patients who were already diagnosed at the State Hospital some of them were absolutely not schizophrenic but were, in fact, so psychotically depressed and so overmedicated that they were relatively dysfunctional to

---

John H. Gagnon, PhD, received his doctorate in clinical psychology from Union Graduate School, Cincinnati, Ohio, in 1982. He is an instructor at the New York Institute for Gestalt Therapy and adjunct professor at Western Connecticut State University.

© 1985 by The Haworth Press, Inc. All rights reserved.

13

begin with and were expected to "get better" on even more major tranquilizers. I knew too little to be certain of my impressions but I did know that lots of medication was the medical treatment of choice both to control behavior and to reduce "terror" (referred to *always* as "anxiety").

When I first settled into the job of program director and allowed myself to actually *see* and *hear* the patients, I began to sense something much larger than the social anxieties of new people meeting one another. I felt the presence of a nameless fear that brought some of those patients to the extreme borders of their creative minds.

It was 1974 and my training was mostly in the behavioral control of unruly patients and the analytic, intellectual, insight approach of psychodynamic psychotherapy so useful with "neurotics." I think that I really *needed* to believe that the appropriate treatment should mostly be behavioral or analytic and that the terror of these patients could simply be "shored up," "held at bay," or "analyzed away." I think I was frightened of losing control of my own emotions and it was frightening for me, therefore, to see others lose control of theirs. In another paper (Gagnon, 1983), I talk about how "right" that loss of control intuitively seemed, however. There was something inherently correct in the notion of letting anyone express exactly what he or she was feeling and I could never totally understand why a patient who kicked over an ashtray would be wrestled to the ground, placed in a wet-sheet-pack and then moved into isolation. Somehow, as frightening as the outburst was, it seemed "right." But as the new director of the Day Treatment Program I was not ready to institute (immediately) what I thought *the* treatment method of choice ought to be for schizophrenic patients. I also did want to impress my supervisor and, mostly, I did want to hold on to my own ordered, rational mind. After all, it was my rational behavior and relative lack of emotional outbursts which distinguished me as the "sane one," the "healer," wasn't it? I was in no way prepared to let myself experience the terror that was to lay ahead for me within the "dark night" of my own mind and I was beginning to dislike these patients because they ever so gently poked at me. They nudged me to feel my intense "hellish" fright: of disorder itself, of going crazy, of doing the "wrong" thing, or of doing something for which God might not forgive me. When I think of this last item I recall how many of these poor patients were tormented by their terror of God. Mary was one of them.

I saw in the eyes of Mary, a pleading, mournful look. A short, heavyset woman of 60 or so, Mary looked more like a very young child about to be beaten mercilessly for something she had done. Mary wanted me to save her, to save her from the "eternal damnation" that would claim her "immortal" soul because she "thought bad words." I tried to help Mary find forgiveness. My own inner "Catholic-boy" shuddered, ran, fled from Mary—from the tortured visions of her believing mind—(from my *own* believing mind). I sometimes cried at night for her when I'd come home. I wanted to help her out of her own damnation (she had left Catholicism and now no longer had a "priest" to forgive her). I think the best times I had with her did occur when I became Mary's "priest." I would gently ask her to tell me the "swear words" that she thought and then I would suggest that God must, in his loving kindness, surely forgive her. These were helpful times both for Mary as well as for me because they let us both do exactly what we needed to do at that time: she be the confessant and I the one with a power to forgive (perhaps even myself someday).

Margaret was different in her religious delusions. She was possessed by "the devil," "Jesus," "God" himself, and her own evil self. All four of these entities spoke to me and to each other at different times. Margaret fought the very primordial biblical battles of light and darkness within herself. Her shattered mind was strewn with the corpses of "peace" and "contentment." Bloody avatars and demons walked among the bodies and torrents of gory, vicious, malicious words poured from Margaret's dried lips. Margaret's terror was of being "dragged down under the ground" where all her relatives "were buried and were still *alive*," like zombies in their small suffocating wooden rooms. Margaret's punishment hung like an executioner's axe, never falling but always threatening. I analyzed Margaret's guilt for the death of her parents. I confronted the ridiculousness of her belief system (at least as *I hoped* it was ridiculous). I rewarded "good" reality testing and supported her occasional flights into meaningful human contact. Margaret improved but only slightly. I don't know if I had any part in this or whether it was due to the medicating job that the staff psychiatrist was doing concurrent to my psychotherapy. Anyway, as time went on, Margaret became less delusional, less frightening, more manageable, and less able to touch my own religious terror.

As the years went by I began to really improve as a therapist. What was at first only a faint glimmer of instinct about "what to do" became a more capable and sensitive skill. I actually began to see a connection between what I experienced in the patient, what I subsequently did or said, and what small improvements I might then witness in the patient. I also had gotten into my own therapy, at first with an analyst, then with a behaviorist, and lastly (and wonderfully) with a Gestalt therapist nearby. George, my dear, new therapist respected me; he respected my thoughts and most of all he respected and supported my emotions. I found myself going through some of the most exciting and terrifying experiences of my entire life right there in the office of this man. I began to realize something. My own terror was sometimes a fear of losing control, so George helped me to lose control. Sometimes, when my terror was "the fear of fear," George let me descend into my own fear to such an extent that entire sessions were taken up lying on his couch screaming as loudly as my lungs would allow. I would come away from the sessions dripping with sweat, completely hoarse, weak with exhaustion, but feeling genuinely relieved, less terrorized, and more trusting of myself.

I began to use what I was learning in my psychotherapy within the work I was doing in my private practice and the results, though at first quite vague, looked promising. I enrolled in the Gestalt Institute of Connecticut and simultaneously took Transactional Analysis at Ridgelea Institute in Stamford, Connecticut. I began to trust more and more in what I could facilitate in a client's process if I mainly learned how to get out of the way, and, as I said before, to trust my own instincts or intuition of what was "needed" in a particular situation. I was convinced that this approach could also work with psychotic patients and I began to discuss these ideas with my staff (Gagnon, 1979). We decided to begin a therapy group in which patients would be allowed to work through their hallucinations and delusions just like people act out scenes in Psychodrama or alone in a Gestalt session (Gagnon, 1981). Bill was one patient who experienced our "new" therapeutic approach.

Bill, a 20-year-old patient, came to the day hospital following his first hospitalization for "acute schizophrenia." In the state mental hospital, Bill had been made less agitated by Haldol therapy. Approximately one year earlier he had undergone surgery for a tumor of the left shoulder. This was his first major illness. He was left with a considerable weakness and a decreased range of motion in his left arm. While he initially showed no schizophrenic or even depressive symptoms, his behavior became increasingly more erratic and bizarre over the following year. He began to hallucinate actively approximately one week prior to mental hospitalization.

When he came to us, Bill complained of visual hallucinations (among other difficulties). After several weeks of orientation to the program, he agreed to work on these hallucinations in a group therapy session. He had already seen some Gestalt therapy work in the program and had some sense of what might be expected of him.

The session began with Bill describing the hallucinations which usually occurred at bedtime and which prevented sleep. He told us he saw "green faces." Hideous and frightening, these images would loom toward him menacingly from the foot of the bed. He became too terrorized to sleep and the images would last for hours. After a lengthy description of the images, Bill was instructed to lie on the floor as if in his bed and to visualize the faces in a chair placed opposite him. He not only imagined them, he told us he clearly saw them and then he became terribly frightened. He was encouraged to talk to the faces and then to get up and play them in whatever way he wished. Although he was, at first, reluctant to change positions and was not forced to move, he voluntarily did switch positions and became the faces. His work proceeded as follows:

Bill: Go away. Leave me alone. (He whimpers and shudders. He repeats this several times and then waits out his reluctance to change positions. With gentle support and coaxing he gets up and moves to the position of the faces.)

Therapist: That's it, Bill. See if you can play the part of the faces for us so *we* can see what they look like. . . . You just play the part.

Faces: Aaaaaagh (a frightening sound, low in the throat). We are here to get you. (His fingers clench. He points the fingers outward like claws.)

Therapist: Can you use your hands even more, Faces? Be aware of what your hands are doing.

Faces: Aaaaagh (He now lunges forward with his "claws").

Therapist: You look like you want to hurt Bill. Do you want to hurt him?

Faces: We want to kill him!! (The therapist repeats this sentence and has Bill change places. He moves back and forth several times between the two positions with the dialogue taking on repeated versions of the same theme: "I want you to leave me alone." vs. "I want to kill you." Finally, he returns once again to the "Bill" position, this time he seems to really *hear* the message from the faces. He appears wide eyed and with a tense body.)

Therapist: O.K., Bill, would you now experience what you are feeling in your body now.

Bill: (He lies down and begins to tremble). Oh No!!!!

Therapist: "Oh no," what, Bill?

Bill: They want to kill me!! (He now looks quite terrified and begins to gurgle a frothy scream in the back of his throat, then looks at the therapist pleadingly.)

Therapist: They want to kill you? . . . You look really scared right now. Would you like some help?

Bill: No, no. I'm not frightened!! (Voice rising in pitch and volume.)

Therapist: (Going with the denial.) O.K. . . . Tell them that. . . . Say, "I'm not frightened of you and I'm not scared of your killing me."

Bill: (Begins mechanically, as if in a trance) I'm not frightened of you. . . . (Suddenly his eyes open wide again and he begins a rising pitched scream. He wraps his arms around himself. The therapist moves forward and experiments with gently holding Bill the same

18 *PSYCHOTHERAPY AND THE TERRORIZED PATIENT*

way he is holding himself. His screaming becomes deeper and louder. His muscles start to relax and he begins to cry heavily. The therapist experiences this as a positive reaction to being held and holds more tightly. Bill's crying goes on for quite a while with him being held tightly throughout. At one point, Bill looks up and screams). . . . The light!!! (The room is dimly lit.) The light. . . . It hurts my eyes. (After Bill reaches a natural calm and he is held and rocked gently for a long time, he sits up with assistance and smiles at us. He also makes clear eye contact.) . . . . I was so scared. I was afraid I *was* dying!

Therapist: Do you think that you are dying now, Bill?

Bill: (After a pause.). . . No. (Smiles.)

Therapist: O.K., Bill. Do you feel like you could do a bit more right now or would you like to stop for today? See how you feel about it.

Bill: (Takes a few minutes to consider this.) Sure. I'm O.K. I'll do a little more.

Therapist: O.K., Bill. Become the faces again if you would.

Bill: (Changes places. His face takes on a more sinister look.)

Therapist: What are you feeling right now?

Faces: I'm evil and deadly . . . but something's different.

Therapist: You're evil and deadly . . . but not to *Bill* anymore?

Faces: Right! But everyone else better watch out because I'm very evil.

Therapist: O.K. Be Bill. (He changes positions.) Do you see the Faces, Bill?

Bill: Not really . . . but I can make believe.

Therapist: (Pleased with the willingness of Bill to ''play'' the evil Faces but also with the fading of the visual hallucinations of them.) O.K. Let's stop here for now. . . .

For one week, Bill reported no hallucinations. We did not, however, have a clear sense of how much integration had occurred. We did see that Bill's fear had decreased considerably and that there was less stress in his ''contact boundary'' (he was able to make better contact with us).

Bill decided to work again several sessions later. The therapist asked him if he would be willing to experiment with the Faces again. He was very willing and was able to make the transition between chairs more easily this time. He actually began to enjoy the power of being the Faces in all of their evilness. This time the therapist asked him to try to frighten other members of the group. He did this gleefully and felt stronger afterward. It was in this playing out of the frightening and aggressive Faces that Bill made tremendous progress. His whole demeanor changed after this. Bill became more energetic and confident. He did not have any further hallucinations and seemed much more lucid.

As time went on Bill still occasionally became disoriented and distant as he spoke. He also denied any connection between the green faces and anything that had actually occurred in his life (like the operating room masks and the "light" over the table on which he had had his cancer surgery one year before.) This did not seem like a necessary piece of insight for him or a target goal for us. The fact was, Bill was now able to sleep at night and was less *terrorized.*

In Gestalt therapy, retroflection is the act of turning an energy, which belongs in the environment, back upon the self (Perls, Goodman, & Hefferline, 1951, pp. 146 ff.). Robert Resnick (1978) says, "Instead of picking on or criticizing you, I pick on or criticize myself." Three years ago, I underwent major surgery in which my left leg was amputated. I went through (and still go through) a tremendous amount of anger, even hatred about what happened to me. When I retroflected this furious, angry energy I became immensely depressed and terrorized (I was terrified of the intensity of my own feelings). When allowed to "feel" my anger and hatred in all its juicy fury, I felt much better (Nichols & Zax, 1977). I don't know much about Bill's background as a child but I think that it is fairly clear that when he retroflected his "evil," murderous side at himself (using the "projected" image of the surgeons in their masks), he could terrify himself into hallucinations but when he "got into" the side of himself that was full of "evil and threatening" energy, Bill was able to own the malevolence, feel more powerful, and be less frightened. When Bill *became* (literally) the Faces he was not a serious threat to others. It seemed that when Bill gave himself permission to "be" all that he was, the intensity of his feelings was much less than expected. Paranoia is often the projection of one's malevolence upon the environment, and the "terror" of the paranoid person comes from imagining that all of the things he'd really like to do to others is not in him at all but is coming from others around him (Perls et al., 1951). Danny was like this:

Danny, a 15-year-old boy, was often withdrawn and fearful, although he could be quite verbal when he wanted to be. He came to me in my private practice at the request of his mother, who felt that Danny's isolation from his peers was not a healthy thing.

Danny believed that he was constantly being stared at. *He* never watched anyone to check out his belief, but he *assumed* that people were always staring at him in a critical way. Occasionally he would look at someone and find that person looking back. Danny would then avert his gaze and

20 PSYCHOTHERAPY AND THE TERRORIZED PATIENT

persist with the idea that he was being stared at. His eyes often appeared glassy and unfocused.

In one session, after several preliminary attempts to make "eye contact" with Danny, I asked him if he was willing to experiment with the use of his eyes.

Therapist: Danny, are you aware that you haven't looked at me at all during this session?

Danny: Uh . . . no. Well, I mean . . . I suppose not.

Therapist: You suppose not?

Danny: Yeah . . . (He begins to fiddle with his fingers) . . . uh . . . I don't like people staring at me. (Finger-movement increases.) It makes me uncomfortable.

Therapist: You feel uncomfortable with *me* right now?

Danny: Yeah. . . . I feel like you hate me or something. I don't know. (He shifts uneasily back and forth in the chair, his eyes averted downward.)

Therapist: Would you be willing to try something?

Danny: What?

Therapist: Would you try looking at me and see what I look like?

Danny: I guess so. . . . Yeah . . . sure. (He raises his eyes up and looks glassily for a moment. Then he appears to become startled and returns his gaze to the floor.)

Therapist: What did you see Danny?

Danny: Nothing much. . . . Just you?

Therapist: Did I look hateful?

Danny: (Nods). . . . A little.

Therapist: Danny, would you try and keep your eyes on me for as long as you can and see me even though I might look hateful right now? You can stop whenever you feel too uncomfortable.

Danny: (Looks up. His eyes again widen and he appears frightened. He still appears unfocused).

Therapist: (Nodding) That's it, Danny. See if you can stay with the looking. Do you feel anything right now?

Danny: Yeah. . . . I feel scared! (The therapist encourages Danny to experience more of his fear, which he does. He attempts to control the emerging feeling by not shaking and by keeping his breathing shallow. The therapist instructs him to be aware of both of these things and he begins to shake more profoundly. After a few moments, Danny begins to cry. His crying keeps up for approximately 5 minutes with shaking and, at times, with deep sobbing. After a while, Danny stops shaking, maintains looking at the therapist and relaxes. His eyes appear to come into focus.)

Therapist: What happened, Danny?

Danny: I was really scared of you I guess, but I feel a little better now. (The session winds down.)

In subsequent sessions Danny was asked to repeat the contact experiment with me and alternately he was successful or was so terrorized that he had to look away for the remainder of the session. After a while I got him to experiment with the notion that people who look at others can make the other person quite uncomfortable. I then "trained" Danny to look at me and when I began to feel a little uncomfortable, I would break the gaze and look away. He began to sense his own power in his eyes. I wanted him to realize that he was projecting his ability to make others feel uncomfortable and that he could take back this power if he wanted. He succeeded very nicely and after a couple of months felt quite comfortable with making eye contact and looking at others. I consider this use of the eyes a form of "grounding" (just like the bioenergetic concept using the feet) (Lowen, 1977, p. 11). Therefore I wanted Danny to learn to ground himself with his eyes.

It took a few years for Danny to become consistently proficient at owning his own personal power but he was able to use his eyes in an "aggressive" way in order to ground himself at will.

This again reminds me of how important "seeing" was for me in my own therapy. For several years my ability to "see" clearly (get grounded through my eyes) was very closely connected to my ability to "feel" my emotions. In other words, I found that when I was in good visual contact externally, I was also in good kinesthetic/emotional contact internally. I often did some of my best "terror" work simply while driving along the road and carefully seeing the trees, the sky, the other cars, and the road. At moments like these, I would suddenly become aware of my own "held down" anger and the fear that accompanied it, and I would pull off to the side of the road where I could safely "go into" the feelings in a powerful way (rage, hit the passenger seat next to me, cry, scream out the fear, etc.). After I did this, I was usually able to continue driving, feeling much more relaxed and in sharp, pleasurable contact with my surroundings.

At this point I am flooded with the names and faces of patients whom I have witnessed in their own, personal terror. Helen, Brad, Terry, Alexandra, Pat, Alan, Karen, Stacey, and many, many more. I think this paper is beginning to get too long, however. It's time for me to tell just one more tale, perhaps an unfinished one, and then to say a little bit about terror from a theoretical perspective.

It is 1984. This past year, just before Christmas, I received a call from a neighboring school system asking me if I would see a student of theirs. A very skilled and talented artist, Tony has a sense of line quality, texture, and shape that I have not before seen in so young an art student. While he had had a successful sophomore year in high school, Tony's behavior has been getting increasingly more erratic. He was withdrawing from his peers and complaining more and more to his art teacher and to the school psychologist about vague and strange sensations ("I feel like gears that don't mesh, like I don't have any gravity, you know, all jagged . . . not smooth at all . . . angular . . . ," etc.) When Tony called for an appointment, I was so struck by the weak, confused quality of his voice that I spent extra time on the phone giving him directions to my office. I even asked him to call me from a phone booth nearby from where I would give him even further directions. On the day of his first appointment I had expected to meet someone who was of below average intelligence. My impression of him over the phone was quite incorrect. What I had heard as mild retardation, turned out to be severe depression. There was also something else. There was that lack of empathy, looseness of association, and spacey, out-of-contact quality that I associate with schizophrenia.

I carefully did an intake session with him and attempted to get some sense of his difficulties. I felt very confused at the end of this first hour. I mostly was aware of how frightened I felt in Tony's presence. He agreed that he would bring in his sketch pad for me to see next week. I told him he could call me in the meantime if there was any serious need.

When Tony brought in his pad and held it out to me I remember feeling aware of wanting to show acceptance of his artwork, whatever the quality. The first few sketches were a total surprise to me. They were beautiful renderings of figure-models and sketches of Tony's father sleeping. The work was so life-like that I was overwhelmed by the sensitivity of this young artist. Suddenly, on the fourth page I began to see the kind of horror which I had only sensed the week before. There on the pages were very realistic sketches of mutilated bodies, of heads with knives through the eyes, bodies covered with feces, heads contorted into grotesque shapes; and on one page was a picture of two young lovers in a gorgeous, sensual, naked embrace. The male lover held her from behind the head, their lips in a voluptuous kiss. The head, however, was severed from her body which lay at the male's feet. In his right hand was the knife.

I was horrified. The work was at the same time beautiful and yet terrifying. I found myself mincing my words about how good the drawing was and completely failing to tell him how disturbed I felt. He was very pleased with my reaction to the drawings. I felt sick to my stomach.

In the next session I was actually able to share with Tony how disturbed I was with some of his work, how frightened it made me feel. He seemed unable to understand and seemed to only react to the possibility that I might not like something that he had done (Tony said to me that he wanted to be the "world's best artist" someday). I now believed that I was dealing with a youth who was beginning the journey into schizophrenic psychosis. I called a local psychiatrist and referred Tony to him for possible medication. This medical colleague agreed with my diagnosis and put Tony on Haldol and Elavil (for the depressive symptoms we were also seeing).

Tony began to get steadily worse. He showed all sorts of bizarre behavior in our sessions, frequently left me feeling frightened for him or his father, and began calling me and the psychiatrist with bizarre, vague complaints. I and the psychiatrist concurred that Tony was ready for hospitalization. I suggested this to Tony in one session and he agreed that it might be helpful. He entered the inpatient service of Danbury Hospital around January. I visited him every couple of days and worked with the staff to coordinate a total treatment for Tony. With his medication regulated, Tony rose up from his depressive state, and we also saw a decrease in his incomprehensible behavior. He was discharged in March and once again is back in therapy with me.

As Tony is being slowly taken off his medication, I have been working with him to deal with the many images of mutilation in his artwork in which the "head" was destroyed. It appears that Tony had wanted to destroy his own head when he found his thoughts becoming increasingly less ordered and sensible. He has come a long way in respecting his own mind but recently has focused upon the idea that his "creativity is totally gone." This, of course, is terribly disturbing to someone who wanted to be the world's best artist. I have begun to interpret the grandiosity and encourage Tony to see himself as valuable even if he is not the best. This at first was totally foreign to him and he resisted and fought to prove to me that he had lost all ability as an artist. (Both his instructors and myself disagree with Tony.) This placed us at existential loggerheads in the therapy. Today, just today, Tony made a breakthrough in this. The session was as follows:

Tony: You say that my artwork still looks creative. But I don't think I'm as creative anymore . . . at least I'm not as creative as I want to be. . . . It's not good enough.

Therapist: O.K. So you're convinced that you have lost your creativity. Can you accept that you are still worthwhile even if you are less creative?

Tony: You want me to accept myself where I am. If I do this, then I am accepting myself as uncreative and I can't do this.

Therapist: That makes sense.

Tony: I can prove that I'm less creative. I can't read philosophy books like I used to. I don't understand the existentialism I used to read.

Therapist: How does not understanding philosophy prove that you are less creative?

Tony: Because creativity *is* the ability to understand anything.

Therapist: That's interesting. I always thought of creativity as the unique way in which someone puts together the elements of a scene or musical composition that makes a personal artistic statement from that person.

Tony: Well. . . . That *is* what creativity is . . . hmmm . . . well. . . . If I'm still creative, then how come I don't see beauty and truth in everything anymore?

Therapist: You don't, huh? Well, neither do I.

Tony: Everything isn't beautiful to you?

Therapist: Nope. In fact today I am particularly struck by how ugly it looks outside with the drizzling rain and all.

Tony: Yeah . . . . (Looking pleased, like he's got me.) But if you don't experience the beauty it is because it is *you* who doesn't see the beauty. It might be very beautiful rain to someone else!

Therapist: Absolutely right. I guess that what I make of how something looks is definitely the result of how I feel inside.

Tony: So if I *feel* uncreative, I might not actually *be* uncreative, it just might be a feeling of mine, a way of how I see things.

Therapist: (Feeling absolutely impressed with this young boy's creative thinking.) That is amazing. I think you have just hit on an explanation for why you experience your artwork as uncreative when your teachers and myself see it as quite creative. In fact, what you just did was creative.

Tony: What do you mean? All I did was think something out.

Therapist: You put what you knew together into a unique combination that brought meaning out of the chaos you had before. I would call that pretty creative.

Tony: Maybe I am creative. . . . (His face is bright and he is smiling.) . . . Maybe I am just looking negatively at who I am!

Therapist: I think that's correct. (I smile at him.)

Tony: You said before that you didn't think that the day was beautiful. Do you ever feel unhappy?

Therapist: Sure. Just this morning I was feeling very sad.

Tony: (Looking unbelieving) How could *you* feel sad?

Therapist: Well, I was feeling the beginning of spring and I was feeling like I was a young animal, ready to run and leap and jump and then I realized how hurt my legs are and how I can't jump or run or leap anymore. I felt very sad having to give up my idea about myself as a young, wild animal. I even cried for a while.

Tony: Wow! That's how I feel. Like I've got to give up the idea that I could be the world's best artist and I don't want to give that up.

Therapist: (Sensing the tremendous empathy that we had finally reached together) I guess you and me will just have to let go and let ourselves mourn our losses. It sure isn't easy, Tony. A lot of times I just want to deny that there is anything less or "imperfect" about me.

Tony: (Nodding very thoughtfully) Yep. Me too. (He smiled very broadly and I felt like this was a major breakthrough for him. Tony was managing to give up a bit of his grandiosity and even though this was hard he seemed to take strength and courage from my own personal losses. We were so intimate and so humanly connected at the close of the session I felt just delighted.)

Tony has a lot more work to do I am sure. Today, however, he was able to realize what it was like to be merely human. I am pleased with this progress and feel hopeful about Tony's replacement of his narcissistic image with a real sense of accomplishment and ability as time goes on (Mahler, 1975). I believe that Tony began to experience the loss of his image and this loss seems to be the very thing that scared him in the past year when he began his trip into depression and psychosis. He would rather have "destroyed his mind" than face the terror of the real world of imperfection, unhappiness, down-feelings, ambiguity, and so forth.

CONCLUSION

There are many reasons why people suffer from terror: For some it may be the fear of a particular feeling, for example, anger. For others there is a fear of the total annihilation of their existence when they violate a basic rule of their family of origin. Some are terrified of experiencing life itself; the feelings, the pleasures are much too awful to endure. For a few individuals, a fear of the "wrath of God" terrorizes them into living a "hell on earth." For another group of people, the conflict that exists within them about some area of life leaves them filled with self-loathing and the fear of their own self-hatred. Retroflections, introjections, projections all keep the terror alive and doing its job to prevent the individual from living life to its fullest, energetically. There are many other individual reasons for feeling terror. I have even experienced the fear of fear in my own life. In some cases the treatment is to undo the irrational constructs that support the unhealthy processes that create terror. In many cases, the *feeling* of the terror is a major step in at least alleviating its grip temporarily.

I enjoy using action-oriented therapies like Gestalt or Psychodrama (Moreno, 1953) to help individuals act through their conflicts and fearful projections. In the last case, with Tony, I found it most helpful to be very intellectual with him and to let him use his bright intellect to figure out what might be true about his belief system or what might be false. Tony did this very well. I also have experienced over the years a tremendous success in using myself throughout the therapeutic process, not only as a facilitator of Gestalt experiments but also as another human being who is present to experience and witness this person in his or her own unique agony. I am very convinced that the personhood of the therapist must be present at every step in the therapy (Kellerman, 1979). To do less is to be a mere technician, treating people like machines. Lastly, I would like to add that I think that therapists who are afraid of terror in others ought to examine their own and face it. It is in this personal journey that the therapist can learn so much valuable information and empathy to use in guiding those others whom we refer to as "the terrorized patients."

REFERENCES

Freedman, A., & Kaplan, H. (1967). *Comprehensive textbook of psychiatry.* Baltimore: Williams & Wilkins.

Gagnon, J.H. (1979). A case of folie a deux in twin sisters and its treatment in a day-hospital setting. *Group Psychotherapy, Psychodrama and Sociometry, 32,* 62-74.

Gagnon, J.H. (1981). Gestalt therapy with the schizophrenic patient. *The Gestalt Journal, 4*(1), 29-46.

Gagnon, J.H. (1983). A personal experience with the institutional reinforcement of retroflection. *VOICES: The Art & Science of Psychotherapy, 19*(1), 57-61.

Kellerman, P.F. (1979). Transference, countertransference and tele. *Group Psychotherapy, Psychodrama and Sociometry, 32,* 38-55.

Lowen, A. (1977). *The way to vibrant health.* New York: Harper Colophon.

Mahler, M. (1975). *The psychological birth of the human infant.* New York: Basic Books.

Moreno, J.L. (1953). *Who shall survive?* (2nd ed.). Beacon, NY: Beacon House.

Nichols, M., & Zax, M. (1977). *Catharsis in psychotherapy.* New York: Garner Press.

Resnick, R. (1978). *Gestalt therapy.* A Psychology Today Cassette. New York: Ziff-Davis.

The Headless Toy Soldiers:
The Terrorization of a Patient
by Unsoothing Introjects

Juana Culhane

This is primarily a brief case presentation of a patient who developed a mild case of systemic lupus erythematosus (also known as SLE or lupus), in the course of her self-psychology-oriented (Kohut, 1971) psychotherapy.

My question, at the outset, is this: What involvement, if any, can an intensive treatment have in the etiology of what seems to be a psychoneuroimmunological disorder (Ader, 1981)?

The question has been stimulated primarily by the work of the Simontons (1975, 1976, 1978). If there is the possibility of curing cancer, which like lupus implicates the immune system, through psychotherapeutic means, then I must ask, is it not possible to cause a disease through the same psychotherapeutic means? Of course, in the latter situation the results would be inadvertent.

The patient, Louise, is a statuesque, robust editorial assistant for a popular magazine. She is in her early 30s and has been in treatment with me for approximately 2 years, with three sessions per week.

When Louise came to her present treatment, she had had 3 years of previous psychotherapy; she had sought help because she was depressed over the breakup of a love affair. Louise sought treatment with me because she was still depressed; she still thought of her lover; she also had no sense of direction, of anticipation, of joy in anything.

Louise said that before and during the time of her love affair she had enjoyed sex and socializing; after her affair was terminated she slowly lost interest in dating and in sex.

Louise knew that this very special love affair had not been good. Nevertheless, she had enjoyed the passion of having expectations, of being torn apart by ambivalences, and even of suffering. Louise said that her lover had been self-centered, domineering, and often insensitive to

---

Juana Culhane is a Fellow of the American Institute for Psychotherapy and Psychoanalysis and a National Certified Counselor. In practice she is a teacher, counselor, lecturer and writer in the area of Psychosocial Rheumatology, and a psychotherapist inspired by self-psychology as taught by Dr. Marjorie T. White.

© 1985 by The Haworth Press, Inc. All rights reserved.

her feelings and thoughts. She had never been sure whether he loved her or not. He would seem to make a move toward her and then he would disappear, retreat; it was like playing hide-and-seek or cat-and-mouse. It had been both exciting and tormenting.

In time, though, this man aroused a gigantic narcissistic rage in her (Kohut, 1972). This quickly led to his leaving her; her state of humiliation, confusion, and emptiness then ensued.

Louise felt that generally, before her affair, she had been a relatively calm, happy woman with hardly any bad things having occurred in her life except for a brother being born when she was five; her mother being so obsessive about her family's appearance, manners, and reputation; her airline-executive father getting tearful and wobbly when he drank; and her severe menstrual cramps from time to time.

Eventually Louise began to remember more about her background. However, she could not remember any actual feelings, only events. Somehow, present experiences, which were filled with emotion, gave her a clue to what she must have felt under similar circumstances in the past. She talked of how she spent most of her energies maintaining a social mask of well-bred gentility, with a veneer of superiority (Miller, 1981), in the areas of female independence and in having a sense of obligation for the less fortunate of this world. Louise also talked of how ashamed she was that she needed psychotherapy and, even worse, that she needed a psychotherapist. Louise revealed, with much difficulty, how humiliated she felt at my changing her appointment when necessary, at her having to pay me, at having to leave when the time was up. Louise had a deep fear that I would leave town, die, or decide that I had had enough of working with her.

Louise thought that she had always been embarrassed by her parents because they were so vulnerable and afraid of the world. She couldn't remember how old she was when she had started to feel that she could not look up to them, idealize them, depend on them for a soothing atmosphere (Cohler, 1980). Louise's parents could not stand any ripples in their lives. She and her brother had to be nice, clean, quiet, and always obedient. Her parents had always favored the brother because he had been able to conform. Louise had the impression she was too active, loud, and somehow disagreeable. In looking back, Louise felt intensely jealous of her brother and of her father because they received so much attention. Her mother catered especially to her father and protected his feelings from being hurt by anyone.

Louise doesn't remember exactly how old she was, perhaps six or seven, when, one evening when the family had gathered together on the front porch, she had taken out a troop of tattered soldiers to play with, and her world had exploded. Where had she gotten the soldiers? What! In return for all of her new, lovely dolls? How could she do this to her loving parents, humiliate and mock them! No daughter of theirs was to be seen playing with such trash! And the soldiers were swept up and thrown away.

Louise could not remember how she had acted or felt, but in her late teens she had written a prize-winning story about some headless toy soldiers who had come to life and attacked the little girl who owned them, and had killed her. The soldiers were angry because she had gone back on her promise to mold new heads for them.

Louise eventually came to see these headless soldiers as introjects of her parents who were displeased at her lack of caring and supportiveness. Louise also felt that she had forfeited her life by not looking after her life-givers properly. She felt she should not have given her soldiers up, that she should have saved them from the garbage.

Louise came to see her love affair as a repetition of her relationship with her parents. The great pain she felt was the sensation that once again she had not cared for her loved one sufficiently well to warrant being loved. In addition, Louise suffered the realization that somehow it was not only the ''other'' whom she had in a sense betrayed and disappointed, but that it was herself. In other words, the soldiers were both her needy parents and also the chosen, treasured objects that represented her divergence and liberation from these parents.

As ''fate'' would have it, Louise's trauma was to be repeated within the treatment.

For several weeks I had been recovering from a leg injury. One day, at the end of a session with Louise, I began to get up from my chair and found, to my horror, that my bad leg was not supporting me adequately. I fell to the floor. Louise looked at me with no expression on her face. She helped me to get up, since I was unable to do so by myself. I brought up the subject at the start of the next session. Louise seemed blank and remote; she said she hardly remembered it. She began to talk about something else.

Within a few months Louise began to develop physical symptoms that were eventually to be diagnosed as lupus. Louise first developed a barely discernible pink rash across the nose and cheeks. Then she felt a vague soreness in her wrists, and in her knees. Her fingers became bluish after only some exposure to the cold, and she developed small ulcers around her mouth.

Louise's family doctor sent her to a rheumatologist. Her tests revealed decreased white cells, depressed red cells, and abnormal autoantibodies.

Lupus is primarily a disorder of the immune system, our physiological defense system. This system protects us by knowing the difference between ''self'' and an intruder, an ''other'' (Locke, 1982). In the case of lupus, the body's defenders turn against the ''self'' and attack healthy connective tissues. In other words, the body's antibodies attack other parts of the body, thus making lupus an autoimmune disease (Fries, 1979). Lupus is often mild but at worst it can lead to nephritis when the autoantibodies form immune complexes which collect inside the kidneys.

Much research indicates that emotional stress affects changes in the immune system (Ader, 1981; Pelletier, 1977).

I then began to wonder if the stress of Louise's treatment was involved in the etiology of her disease. Of course, other factors are thought to be involved: genetic predisposition, the possibility of a virus triggering off the confusion of the immune system; a low tolerance for traumas; a learned emotional restrictiveness (Stephanos, 1980); or a lack of commitment to life, to the self (Totman, 1979).

Of course, stress is a biological necessity. It can be both good and bad; what seems to matter is whether we perceive stressors to be stressful or not. However, when there is a stress reaction and it is chronic and prolonged, it can weaken the immune system (Pelletier, 1977).

Certainly, in Louise's case, the particular stressors could be construed to be the introjects of her parents and/or the continuing reawakening of these introjects through important self-objects.

It became essential that Louise and I work through the falling incident (White, 1982). I again opened up the subject. After much prodding, she said that she thought she had been very angry with me for needing her help, for my being so vulnerable. Soon she was consumed with different feelings. She dreaded the possibility that she had neglected to look after me properly, to listen to me, to learn, to work hard. Louise also thought she might have gotten to be too much for me, that she was too unendingly unwell.

Louise also worried that her rage at not having gotten affirmed, appreciated, and encouraged as a growing individual would spill over onto me, and that I would not be able to accept her as she was.

In fantasy, Louise tossed my furniture around the room; she rummaged through my desk and file drawers, ferreting out all of my secrets and shames; she destroyed all references to other patients; she attacked me sexually and forced me to find pleasure in her arms; and finally she imagined herself sitting on my lap, at age 13 months, facing me, touching my face, my features, with wonder, and enjoying the strength of my hands on her back, holding her up.

Louise's lupus seems to be under control for the moment, according to her rheumatologist.

This, of course, can be seen as proof of nothing. The disease may return in its original, mild form, or in a fully unfurled form, or it may never show up again. Whatever happens, we will again have to take a guess as to why it has come about. Still, I don't see how we can ever imagine the mind or the body being separately and individually omnipotent. It is obvious that the interactions among environmental factors, the hypothalamus, the immune system, the endocrinology system, all attest to the compact unity we have always been.

Louise has tried, and is trying, to build some heads for her soldiers. In her eyes, they are not good enough yet. However, Louise knows that she alone had obtained these figures; they were her very own. She would never again give them up to the garbage; and one day she would even make them complete.

REFERENCES

Ader, R. (Ed.). (1981). *Psychoneuroimmunology.* New York: Academic Press.

Cohler, B.J. (1980). Developmental perspectives in the psychology of the self in early childhood. In A. Goldberg (Ed.), *Advances in self psychology.* New York: International Universities Press.

Fries, J.F. (1979). *Arthritis: A comprehensive guide.* Reading, MA: Addison-Wesley.

Kohut, H. (1971). *The analysis of the self.* New York: International Universities Press.

Kohut, H. (1972). Thoughts on narcissism and narcissistic rage. *The psychoanalytic study of the child,* Vol. 27. New York: International Universities Press.

Locke, S.E. (1982, April 24-25). *Stress, coping and human immunity.* Conference sponsored by the Institute for Psychosocial Study, New York City.

Miller, A. (1981). *Prisoners of childhood.* New York: Basic Books.

Pelletier, K.R. (1977). *Mind as healer, mind as slayer. A holistic approach to preventing stress disorders.* New York: Delta.

Simonton, O.C., Simonton, S., & Creighton, J.L. (1978). *Getting well again.* New York: Bantam Books.

Stephanos, S. (1980). Analytical psychosomatics in internal medicine. *International Journal of Psycho-Analysis, 7,* 219-232.

Totman, R. (1979). *Social causes of illness.* New York: Pantheon.

Power and Terror of Change

Lawrence Tirnauer

Patients are generally much more terrified than we realize. Fully one-half to two-thirds of my patients have been themselves, or had a parent, sibling, or child who has been psychiatrically hospitalized, actively and seriously suicidal, seriously sexually abused, or had a serious addiction problem. Patients have learned to hide this terror, because parents, friends, and professionals are often frightened by the person who appears terrified. Often this terror only comes out in dreams and nightmares, in reaction to certain drugs, or in the later stages of intensive psychotherapy. Patients then rightly fear that the loosening of defenses will bring them to a much more dangerous and frightening place in their lives. Symptoms often represent the patients' attempt to work out some compromise about some terrifying aspect in their lives. In this paper, I have attempted to focus on how fear and power are inextricably intertwined.

PARAMETERS OF POWER

Issues of power are so diverse and complex that one is soon forced to narrow one's focus or end up feeling overwhelmed by this very complexity. Power is related to *control,* and control can be used constructively or destructively. Feelings of power are related to feelings of helplessness, and so it is difficult to talk about one without the other.

Power is varied. One can talk of the power of understanding, or the power of intimacy, or the power of confrontiveness, just as one can talk of the power of confusion, the power of helplessness, or the power of masochism. Similarly power can be used to facilitate the growth of another person, just as power can be used against another person. And as one person's power can be experienced positively, so power can be experienced as abusive or threatening by another person.

Lawrence Tirnauer, PhD from the Pennsylvania State University, is engaged in the private practice of psychotherapy in Washington, D.C. This article is based on a panel presentation by Dr. Tirnauer at the annual conference of the American Academy of Psychotherapists in Chicago in October 1984. He is president-elect of the American Academy of Psychotherapists.

© 1985 by The Haworth Press, Inc. All rights reserved.

CULTURAL IMPERATIVES

In this culture power is often seen as having a confrontive or macho quality. Western culture emphasizes a kind of mastery and perfectionism. In the Orient power is often related to the ability to be flexible and yielding. There, incompleteness and imperfection are often more highly valued as an inherent part of the nature of the human condition, if not the very nature of the universe. *Both* are valuable and there are times when a psychotherapist needs to be very aggressive and insistent. For example, some patients need to feel this aggressiveness in order to feel that the therapist is really interested or can be genuinely trusted.

ESSENTIALS OF POWER

For the psychotherapist, an awareness of the complexities of power helps preserve the integrity of the therapeutic relationship: First are the many aspects of power that either patient or therapist may experience as *abusive.* Second is the other side of power: those feelings of helplessness in the therapy relationship. Finally, and because it has great relevance to issues of both helplessness and abuse, is projective defensiveness.

THE POWER OF TERROR

Patients have an enormous terror of both psychotherapy and psychotherapists. This is not because either is necessarily punitive. Good therapy is, by its very nature, a threat to the identity of the patient. This identity includes his or her defenses with their accompanying means of protection and any deeper sense of his or her truer self. These defenses have usually protected patients from more disastrous outcomes and interactions as they were growing up. For example, the patient's most vindictive, hateful, paranoid, or confused life-style needs to be seen when possible as a defense against an unbelievably punitive superego, one which if unleashed might well drive the patient to suicide. At other times these defenses need to be seen as a bulwark against what feels for the patient like a complete loss of ego boundaries, thus leading to psychosis. In such cases the patient is rightly terrified by the therapist's well-meaning attempts at understanding and contact. Attempts to bring about change rightly carry with them the fear of a *worse* outcome, not just a more positive one. The therapist is probably not free from such fears despite intensive training and personal therapy. As psychotherapy evolves with any given patient it inherently forces the therapist to face all those neglected, immature, painful, alien, and ineffectual aspects of his or her own personality. Such aspects are part and parcel of being a human being, as are fears of grief, abandonment, criticism, homosexuality, murderousness, and seductiveness.

THE PURSUIT OF POWER

Although the therapist's power may be welcomed by the patient, yet for its own sake it is inherently self-defeating. And while welcomed by the patient, it is also seen as a threat. For example, the therapist's understanding can be seen by the patient as highlighting a lack of understanding, or depriving the patient of finding his or her own answers. The therapist's "lovingness" may be seen by the patient as competitive—highlighting the patient's own cruelty or indifference. Such power may suggest that negative feelings toward the therapist are not welcome. In fact, there is no way that any course the therapist takes may not be seen by the patient as a threat. Nevertheless, rather than serving as a cause for discouragement, this kind of awareness opens the door to helping the patient explore many feelings that may at times seem unacceptable or simply confusing.

Going another step, the pursuit of "power" means cutting off feelings of anxiety, impotence, and helplessness. When they are valued, such feelings provide much useful information for both patient and therapist. If a therapist consistently appears powerful, it is probable that he or she is highly defended against dependent feelings. What is important is that therapists allow themselves to have the courage to let thoughts and feelings unfold as they really are, and not force them to assume some quality that they think they ought to have. Owning up to this, let it be said that no therapist is free from sensitivity to criticism or from fear of depression and/or craziness.

POWER AND ABUSE

Working with seriously depressed and schizoid individuals, one soon discovers that there are many things that patients experience as abusive, some of which are not so readily apparent. Being aware that the patient may experience them as abusive often helps to clarify the basis on which the patient may feel abused, or retaliate by being abusive to the therapist. For example, the moment the therapist enters the waiting room, the therapist's neutrality may be experienced by the patient as indifference, and this may lead the patient to react as if the therapist doesn't care. In so doing, the patient may fear having led the therapist to begin to react in an uncaring way. If the therapist is especially friendly, the terror in the patient may experience this as a criticism of the patient's unhappiness or irritability or seriousness. If the therapist seems a bit depressed or serious when entering the waiting room the patient may experience this as criticism or evidence of his or her own destructiveness. Therapists need to be aware that patients are often extremely sensitive to these subtle attitudes, and *any* demeanor may be experienced as critical or abusive by the patient.

Within the therapy hour the patient may experience the therapist's wish for contact with the patient as an attempt at seduction, or an attempt to exploit the now-terrorized patient. The therapist's request for more information may be experienced as criticism for what was incomplete in his or her story. Likewise the patient may experience the therapist's attempt to help him or her get more in touch with feelings as the therapist's desire to control or invade these feelings. A patient recently told me how enraged he would become when his mother asked him what seemed like simple questions, but which he felt were subtle put-downs and attempts to control him. This led me to think of my own competitiveness with the patient, and my envy of some of his recent activities, rather than merely siding with him about how difficult his mother was.

I am not suggesting that the therapist needs to be less than spontaneous. That would betray the enormous complexity of the therapeutic situation. The therapist needs to be open to seeing his or her own behavior through many different viewpoints. Without such perspective, the therapist may be inclined to feel victimized or abused by the patient and thus react sadistically, without understanding what the patient is in fact reacting to.

HELPLESSNESS AND POWER

Feelings of helplessness are an inherent part of any intense psychotherapy relationship. The therapist who denies this is being less than truthful. Feelings of helplessness may be a necessary defense against other more frightening feelings. Here we need think only of the nightmare. Feelings of helplessness may be a defense against hateful feelings or loving feelings—or dependent feelings or the wish to control the patient. Feelings of helplessness may be a defense against *any* feelings that either patient or therapist believes to be unacceptable in themselves, or in the context of the relationship to each other. Often the only way the therapist can begin to become aware of what the patient is defending against is by first allowing his or her own helpless feelings to surface. Only then is it possible to become aware of what is being defended against. By pursuing some image of power the therapist—as does the patient—cuts self off from this greater awareness.

Both patient and therapist struggle with strong tendencies toward omnipotence and omniscience. These wishes are *never* entirely given up. This in part is because they often lead to positive developments such as a certain knowingness or effectiveness in dealing with the world. On the other hand, they could lead to unrealistic and perfectionistic demands. As the patient, and to varying degrees the therapist, give up some of the compulsive need to understand, the compulsive need to control, the compulsive need to be in touch with one's feelings, or the compulsive need to deal effectively with most situations, feelings of helplessness will probably ensue. Therefore the sometime need to welcome the development of helpless feelings in either patient or therapist. The compulsive need to be powerful can be seen as a defense against this kind of necessary evolution in the therapy relationship.

PROJECTION AND HELPLESSNESS

Initially we may be inclined to think of *projection* as a negative defense. Actually projection serves many constructive purposes, accounting for some of its tenacity. The new patient is inclined to project much of his or her own power onto the therapist. And then, so often it may seem to the therapist, to reduce this helping role to one of helplessness. Nevertheless, projecting this power onto the therapist allows the patient to have the confidence necessary to enter the arduous task of therapy. The patient tends to project onto the therapist his or her own loving and caring feelings, thus allowing the patient the ability to develop the necessary trust in the initial phases of contact so that therapy may begin.

Even as the patient initially projects positive qualities onto the therapist, the therapist may similarly project his or her own positive feelings onto the patient. Such projections help the therapist to have the needed caring necessary in the initial stages of psychotherapy. This process is not unlike the initial phases of a romantic relationship. Later, as therapy progresses, the patient begins to project negative facets onto the therapist, and vice versa. As therapists know from their work with couples involved in high degrees of blaming, this negative projection serves to protect the individual from similar levels of self-punitive blame and guilt.

It is the therapist's ability to tolerate *some* of this negative projection that allows the patient to begin to tolerate and accept these disowned aspects of self. This is not easy. I am convinced that one patient began an extramarital affair with a depressed woman because I could not sufficiently let myself feel the depressed and homosexual feelings he needed to experience in our relationship. It takes a great deal on the therapist's part to be the target for such projections, otherwise he or she might be considered simply masochistic. Negative projections tend to arise at *the very moment* when the patient begins to experience something new and seemingly alien within himself or herself. One patient began his session quite critical of my seeming lack of caring about him. Further examination revealed the patient had been feeling suicidal over the weekend, so that any lack of caring on my part felt quite magnified to him. Further exploration revealed that the patient had been quite critical and "uncaring" of his mother over the weekend. So my relative comfort with being seen as an uncaring person was a necessary development for the patient to come to experience what he sensed was his own lack of caring. In fact he was actually at an early stage of forging a more separate sense of his own identity, one free from that of his mother, with whom he was quite over-identified.

COMBINED POWER AND HELPLESSNESS

Psychotherapists must be comfortable letting themselves experience high degrees of power, as well as high degrees of helplessness. It is essential that therapists develop comfort in letting themselves be experienced as abusive persons as well as caring ones.

None of these tasks are easy. To tolerate these kinds of developments requires a fairly positive sense of self nourishcd by support from colleagues.

The Psychotherapy Patient and the Initial Session: What to Do with the Emotional State

Alvin R. Mahrer
Henry P. Edwards
Gary M. Durak
Irit Sterner

The terrorized patient is representative of those who are in a genuine emotional state in the initial session. Faced with this state, what happens when the therapist uses the common strategy of gathering background information? Critics of this common strategy have raised serious questions of the effects of such a tactic (Beier, 1966; Davis, 1971; Frank, 1959, 1961a, 1961b; Haley, 1963; Labov & Fanshel, 1977; Mahrer, 1983; Stieper & Wiener, 1965).

They argue that patients are forced into the role of information-provider to such an extent that there is a sharp restriction on both the range of what is talked about and the kind of relationship that is established with the therapist. Their arguments favor an alternative strategy in which the therapist facilitates the expression of the patient's immediate presenting condition, problem, or personality-behavioral state, with little or no gathering of problem-related background information.

The first purpose of the study is to provide some empirical data on the

---

Alvin R. Mahrer, Ph.D. from Ohio State University in 1954, is Professor of Psychology, School of Psychology, University of Ottawa, Ottawa, Ontario, Canada K1N 6N5.

Henry P. Edwards completed his doctoral studies in 1967 at the University of Ottawa. He is Director of the Professional Program, School of Psychology, University of Ottawa.

Gary M. Durak, Ph.D. in clinical psychology from University of Ottawa in 1980, is Staff Psychologist, Porter-Starke Services, 701 Wall Street, Valparaiso, IN 46383.

Irit Sterner is a doctoral candidate in the Professional Program, School of Psychology, University of Ottawa.

Grateful appreciation is extended to the members of the Psychotherapy Research Team for their role in each phase of the study.

© 1985 by The Haworth Press, Inc. All rights reserved.

patient effects of emphasizing the gathering of problem-related background information. To our knowledge, the closest related study (Frank & Sweetland, 1962) used a psychotherapy-analogue design in which graduate students interviewed volunteer subjects and patients, and the results confirmed the above criticisms. Yet there are no empirical data on which to assess the efficacy of the common strategy, its criticisms, or alternative strategies. The second purpose is to use these empirical findings as a basis for proposing possible modifications in a strategy dedicated toward gathering problem-related background information, and also to discuss an alternative strategy in the light of the findings.

On the basis of these two purposes, a research design was developed in which actual patients were seen in initial sessions by an exemplar therapist whose approach favored the explicit gathering of problem-related background information. In order to examine patient effects, three hypotheses were investigated. These hypotheses were derived from the widely used strategy of gathering problem-related background information, and the alternative strategy of facilitating the expression of patients' immediate presenting conditions, problems, or personality-behavioral states.

When the therapist emphasizes the gathering of background information, both the standard strategy and the alternative strategy would suggest that the patient's predominant immediate response tendency would be that of providing the requested information. Conspicuous as this hypothesis is, there is no research on the extent to which patients do indeed respond by providing the requested information.

The second hypothesis is that the emphasizing of problem-related background information generates a dyadic interaction in which therapists and patients mutually invite one another to be information-requesters and information-providers. Specifically, it is predicted that (a) therapists selectively request background information when patients are already providing such information, and (b) their patients will provide background information whether or not it is requested by the therapist; that is, both before and after the therapist requests background information, patients will show the same distribution of statements predominated by the providing of background information.

The third hypothesis is generated from criticisms that the requesting of background information discloses a picture of the patient different from that disclosed by other therapist procedures. While it may be expected that differences would occur in the sheer provision of problem-related background information, the hypothesis is that over a series of response categories there will occur significant differences in patients' responses following a therapist's requesting background information as compared with the distribution following all other therapist statements.

METHOD

Therapist and Patients

Selection of a therapist was determined by the availability of verbatim transcripts of initial sessions with patients representing different clinical populations, conducted by a therapist whose approach expressly favors an emphasis on gathering background information on presenting problems. On the basis of these two considerations, the selected therapist was Dr. Joseph Wolpe whose behavioral approach expressly highlights the importance of using the initial session for the gathering of background information on presenting problems (Locke, 1971; Wolpe, 1958, 1969; Wolpe & Lazarus, 1966).

Ideally, the patients would be those in a strong emotional state, for example, in or ready to be in a state of terror. Given the unavailability of such ideal patients' verbatim transcripts with information-gathering therapists, case 1 was an hypochondriacal neurosis in a middle-aged male whose presenting complaints centered upon pains in the arms and chest, and fears of dying of a heart attack (Wolpe, 1976a). Case 2 was a middle-aged hospitalized woman diagnosed as depression related to guilt around sexuality and fear of people (Wolpe, 1976b). Case 3 was a 34-year-old woman diagnosed as anxiety neurosis (Wolpe, 1976b).

Categories of Therapist Statements

Information-gathering about the problem. The therapist gathers information about the problem by asking direct questions about the problem, about the onset and history of the problem, about the nature of the problem, and about the patient's feelings and reactions to the problem.

All other. For the purposes of the study, this single pooled category was sufficient. However, to assist judges in identifying other categories of therapist statements, examples were provided from a number of systems for classifying therapist statements (Kiesler, 1973).

Categories of Patient Statements

Patient statements were placed into a threefold system initially used in psychotherapy research by Seeman (1949) and common to many current systems for classifying client statements (Kiesler, 1973). The three major categories and five subcategories were taken from the systems of Bales (1970), Dollard and Auld (1959), Klein, Mattieu, Gendlin and Kiesler (1970), Murray (1956), Snyder (1945), Stiles (1979), and Truax and Carkhuff (1967).

Self-centered. The patient's statement is predominantly centered upon oneself rather than on the therapist or something external. The two subcategories are: (a) *Problem-Related Information:* The patient provides information about the problem, the nature of the problem, the patient's reactions to or feelings about the problem, the history of the problem, the conditions and circumstances of its occurrence. (b) *Self-Description:* The patient describes and talks about oneself, the kind of person one is, one's behaviors and feelings, exclusive of providing information about the problem.

Therapist-centered. The patient's statement is predominantly centered upon the therapist rather than on oneself or something external. The three subcategories are: (a) *Negative Relationship:* The patient opposes and resists the therapist and the therapist's statement. (b) *Positive Relationship:* The patient accepts and welcomes the therapist and the therapist's statement. (c) *Clarification:* The patient clarifies or seeks neutral understanding of what the therapist says.

External-centered. The patient's statements are predominantly centered upon external situations, figures, or objects rather than on oneself or the therapist. In so doing, the patient is not providing information about the problem.

Procedure

The unit of analysis was the complete statement, consisting of all words spoken in a given interchange by therapist or patient, preceded and followed respectively by the words of the other. Categorization of all therapist and patient statements was done by two clinical psychologists and seven graduate students in clinical psychology.

The nine judges met weekly as a group. In the initial 2-hour meeting, the category system, including verbatim examples from protocols not used in the present study, was explained and discussed. Beginning with the second meeting and thereafter at weekly intervals, judges were given two pages of transcript to place into categories, beginning with case 1 and proceeding sequentially through case 3.

Categorizations were done independently by each judge. Each therapist or patient statement was judged as falling in one of the two therapist categories or one of the six patient categories. The categorizations for the two pages of transcript were collated at weekly meetings, and the next two pages of transcript were assigned. Minimum criterion for agreement among the nine judges was set at 67%.

Each patient statement was treated as either antecedent or consequent to the two classes of therapist statements. Accordingly, each patient statement served both as antecedent to the next therapist statement and consequent to the prior therapist statement.

RESULTS AND DISCUSSION

For case 1, 205 out of 224 (92%) therapist and patient statements met the criterion of agreement. For case 2, 137 of 151 (91%), and for case 3, 214 of 240 (89%) statements met criterion. Although the criterion was 67% agreement among the nine judges, the observed mean percentage of agreement was 87.6% for the 556 statements which reached criterion. The remaining statements were recategorized by the nine judges, and 13 statements, which failed to reach criterion on the second round of categorizations (six in case 1, three in case 2, and four in case 3), were deleted from further analysis. Accordingly, of 615 therapist and patient statements in the three interviews, 602 (97.9%) reached or exceeded criterion and constituted the data.

As a check on the proportion of therapist statements which were categorized as gathering background information on the presenting problems, in cases 1-3, 103 (72%), 42 (59%), and 85 (75%) of all therapist statements were judged as falling into the target category. Accordingly, as indicated in Wolpe's approach, the preponderant therapist statement in the initial interviews for all patients was the target statement. These three sessions may then be taken as representative of Wolpe's use of this procedure.

The second check was to assess whether or not the distributions of patient responses were similar or different over the six categories of patient responses. A comparison of these three distributions over the six categories yielded a Chi-square of 6.32 (df = 5, p > .20), allowing the distributions to be pooled for statistical analysis.

Patients' Responses to Requests for Background Information

How do patients respond when the therapist requests background information? Will the predominant response be that of providing the requested information? To what extent will patients respond by providing the requested information? As given in Table 1, the predominant response is that of providing the requested information, and this comprises almost half (41.0%) of the patients' responses, with self-description and externally centered statements comprising 28.7% and 20.5% respectively. Comparison of these descriptive statistics with other distributions occurs in relation to other hypotheses.

Selective Use of Therapist's Requesting Background Information

The hypothesis is that the therapist will selectively request background information when the patients are already providing such information. If the frequency of patient statements antecedent to therapist information-

44 PSYCHOTHERAPY AND THE TERRORIZED PATIENT

Table 1. Client Statements Antecedent and Consequent to two Categories of Therapist Statements in Three Initial Interviews.

Category of Client Statement	Therapist Requests Problem-Related Information N = 230		All Other Therapist Statements N = 372	
	Antecedent	Consequent	Antecedent	Consequent
Negative Relation to T	2.6	2.5	11.7	10.0
Positive Relation to T	10.3	5.4	10.3	20.5
Clarification of Statement	1.2	1.9	4.8	2.5
Self-Description	26.5	28.7	26.7	19.0
Problem-Related Information	39.6	41.0	24.5	24.9
External Centered	19.8	20.5	22.0	23.1
Column %	100.0	100.0	100.0	100.0

gathering statements is compared with the frequency of patient statements antecedent to all other therapist statements (i.e., columns 1 and 3, Table 1), there is a significant difference (Chi-square 19.86, df = 5, p < .01). The findings suggest that the therapist tends to request background information when patients are already providing background information, as hypothesized; in addition, the findings suggest that the therapist tends to request background information when patients are not engaging in a negative relationship toward the therapist.

Stability of Patients' Role of Information-Providers

The hypothesis is that patients will provide background information whether or not it is requested by the therapist; that is, both before and after the therapist requests background information, patients will show the same distribution of statements predominated by the providing of background information. A comparison of the frequency distributions of patient statements antecedent and consequent to therapist's requests for background information (columns 1 and 2, Table 1) yields a nonsignificant Chi-square of 4.79 (df = 5, p > .10). Both before and after the target therapist statement, the preponderant patient statement was that of providing problem-related background information (39.6% and 41.0% respectively). The findings indicate that both before and after the therapist requests background information, the patients show the same distribution of statements predominated by the providing of problem-related background information.

Differential Distributions of Patients' Responses

The hypothesis is that significant differences will occur between the distribution of patients' responses following the therapist's requesting background information and the distribution of patient responses following all other therapist statements; these differences will occur not only with regard to the patients' tendency to respond by providing the requested problem-related background information, but in other categories of responses as well. When the response distribution consequent to the therapist's requesting of problem-related background information is compared with the response distribution consequent to all other therapist statements (columns 2 and 4, Table 1), a highly significant difference was obtained (Chi-square = 26.01, df = 5, p < .001). Closer inspection of the findings reveals that consequent to all other therapist statements the patients not only seemed to provide less problem-related background information, but also seemed to provide less self-description and more statements indicative of both a positive and negative relationship with the therapist.

Proposed Modifications in Initial Session Strategies

These findings lend themselves to implications both for an initial-session strategy which emphasizes the gathering of problem-related background information, and also for an initial-session strategy facilitating the expression of immediate presenting condition, problem, personality-behavioral state. Each of these shall be described in turn.

For a strategy favoring the gathering of problem-related background information, the findings suggest that patients may be quite cordial to providing background information even when the therapist does not explicitly request such information. The findings also indicate that even when the therapist selectively requests background information when patients are already providing such information, the consequence is not impressively efficient; less than half of the patients' responses (41.0%) consist of the providing of problem-related background information. Finally, when the therapist departed from the requesting of background information, the patients not only provided significantly less background information but also less self-description in general.

On the basis of this interpretation of the findings, three modifications may be proposed in the strategy of gathering problem-related background information. One is that therapists request the relevant background information on a more general basis rather than selectively when patients are already providing such information. Second, it is proposed that therapists cultivate patients' apparent cordiality toward providing background information even when it is not explicitly requested by the therapist. Finally, it is proposed that the gathering of relevant background information serve as the explicitly dominant aim of the initial sessions. Whereas only 38.2% of the therapist's statements were directed toward eliciting such information, the proposal is that a larger proportion of the therapist's statements be directly aimed at acquiring the background picture of the presenting problem.

On the other hand, the findings also lend themselves to interpretation by critics of the above strategy and proponents of a strategy favoring the facilitated expression of the patient's immediate presenting condition, problem, personality-behavioral state. When therapists use a high proportion of requests for background information, and especially when therapists do so on a selective basis, the effect on patients may be interpreted as encompassing them in the constricted role of information-providers. According to this interpretation, patients become locked into a dyadic back-and-forth interaction in which they are information-providers to the therapists as information-requesters. This role relationship prevents the patient from expressing the immediate condition, problem, or personality-behavioral state, and discloses a one-sided picture of the patient's presenting problem and background while depriving both patient and therapist of clinical material relative to self-description, to the nature of their relationship, and perhaps to other aspects of the patient's immediate condition, problem, and personality-behavioral state. When the findings are interpreted from this perspective, there is strong support for arguments against gathering background information (cf. Beier, 1966; Davis, 1971; Frank, 1959, 1961a, 1961b; Haley, 1963; Labov & Fanshel, 1977; Mahrer, 1983; Stieper & Wiener, 1965).

Accordingly, a second proposal is to facilitate the emotional state, to enable it to carry forward. The significant data consist of the having and undergoing of the emotional state rather than background information. It is the terror, the patient who is in the state of terror, rather than background information which is either standard or geared to the "presenting problem." On the basis of this second strategy, the therapist accepts as primary the emotional state, the terror, or whatever it is. The therapist starts with the patient who is in this state, and does whatever the therapist holds as therapeutic with this state. It is opened up, carried forward, enabled to occur. Indeed, the general rule of this strategy is to work with whatever emotional state is here, even and especially in the initial session. To force the patient into the role of information-provider is to suffocate the patient, to twist the patient out of the present state and force the patient to conform to the role-relationship imposed by the therapist.

In summary, the findings provide empirical data on patient effects when the therapist emphasizes the use of the initial session for the explicit gathering of background information on the presenting problem. On the basis of these findings, some modifications may be proposed to improve the gathering of such information under this strategy. In addition, the findings also lend themselves to interpretation from the perspective of an alternative initial session strategy which emphasizes the facilitated expression of the patient's immediate presenting problem, condition, and personality-behavioral state.

REFERENCES

Bales, R.F. (1970). *Personality and interpersonal behavior.* New York: Holt, Rinehart & Winston.

Beier, E.G. (1966). *The silent language of psychotherapy.* Chicago: Aldine.

Davis, J.D. (1971). *The interview as arena.* Stanford, CA: Stanford University Press.

Dollard, J., & Auld, F., Jr. (1959). *Scoring human indices: A manual.* New Haven, CT: Yale University Press.

Frank, J.D. (1959). The dynamics of the psychotherapeutic relationship: Determinants and effects of the therapist's influence. *Psychiatry, 22,* 17-39.

Frank, J.D. (1961a). *Persuasion and healing: A comparative study of psychotherapy.* Baltimore: Johns Hopkins University Press.

Frank, J.D. (1961b). The role of influence in psychotherapy. In M.I. Stern (Ed.), *Contemporary psychotherapies* (pp. 17-41). New York: The Free Press of Glencoe.

Frank, G.H. & Sweetland, A. (1962). A study of the process of psychotherapy. *Journal of Consulting Psychology, 26,* 135-138.

Haley, J. (1963). *Strategies of psychotherapy.* (1963). New York: Grune & Stratton.

Kiesler, D.J. (1973). *The process of psychotherapy: Empirical foundations and systems of analysis.* Chicago: Aldine.

Klein, G.H., Matthieu, P.L., Gendlin, E.T., & Kiesler, D.J. (1970). *The experiencing scale: A research and training manual.* Madison: Wisconsin Psychiatric Institute.

Labov, W., & Fanshel, D. (1977). *Therapeutic discourse: Psychotherapy as conversation.* New York: Academic Press.

Locke, E.A. (1971). Is "Behavior Therapy" behavioristic? (An analysis of Wolpe's psychotherapeutic methods). *Psychological Bulletin, 76,* 318-327.

Mahrer, A.R. (1983). *Experiential psychotherapy: Basic practices.* New York: Brunner/Mazel.

Murray, E.J. (1956). A content analysis method for studying psychotherapy. *Psychological Monographs, 13* (whole number 420).

Snyder, W.U. (1945). An investigation of the nature of non-directive psychotherapy. *Journal of General Psychology, 33,* 193-223.

Stieper, D.R., & Wiener, D.N. (1965). *Dimensions of psychotherapy: An experimental and clinical approach.* Chicago: Aldine.

Stiles, W.B. (1979). Verbal response modes and psychotherapeutic techniques. *Psychiatry, 42,* 49-62.

Truax, C.B., & Carkhuff, R.R. (1967). *Toward effective counselling and psychotherapy: Training and practice.* Chicago: Aldine.

Wolpe, J. (1958). *Psychotherapy by reciprocal inhibition.* Stanford, CA: Stanford University Press.

Wolpe, J. (1969). *The practice of behavior therapy.* New York: Pergamon.

Wolpe, J. (1976a). Initial interview in a hypochondriacal neurosis. In A. Wandersman, P. Poppen & D. Ricks (Eds.), *Humanism and behaviorism: Dialogue and growth* (pp. 97-108). New York: Pergamon.

Wolpe, J. (1976b). *Theme and variations: A behavior therapy casebook.* New York: Pergamon.

Wolpe, J., & Lazarus, A. (1966). *Behavior therapy techniques.* New York: Pergamon.

Primitive Agonies

Elizabeth M. Ellis

In a lifetime we will each experience a great many fears. Most will be situation-specific and hopefully transient. Some will last and become a deep-rooted and pervasive influence on our lives. Still others will be so interwoven with the fabric of our personality and our general view of the world that we hardly know they are there. As psychotherapists we grow accustomed to hearing about people's fears. There are fears of rejection, fears of failure, fears of loss of approval, fears of loss of one's loved ones, fears of making a fool of oneself. These are garden variety fears, the stock in trade of the psychotherapist.

Then there are those fears which have a quality of mystery about them, dark and inchoate. They are like the creatures from high-school biology textbooks whose fins evolved into legs during a drought and they heaved themselves up out of the primeval muck and lay belly down on the swampy shore gasping for breath. These fears are like distant relatives out of our prehistoric past. Most of us experienced them in our own individual histories at one time or another. We have a vague sense of knowing these relatives but we don't know their names and we find it rather unpleasant to be reminded of them.

Yet psychotherapists know them. With experience we will hear of them over and over again. At times a client will be astounded that we can know what the unknown fear is, not that we can define it perhaps, but at least we can describe it. And if we're really good, we can describe it with an awareness, drawn from our own past, of what it is like to feel the fear. These are chthonic fears, meaning dark, under the earth, as in the Greek deities of the underworld. These are primitive fears. These are fears that lie at the very heart of us, fears that dwell behind the surface fears that we present to the world. Some would call these schizoid fears. Perhaps so. Yet I believe we have all experienced them at one time and may experience them again to greater or lesser degrees. I have grouped them under six headings.

(1) Fear of being abandoned. We are social creatures. Some say we were made to live in twos, or threes, or fours. It comes as no surprise that

---

Elizabeth M. Ellis received her PhD in clinical psychology from Emory University in 1977. She maintains an independent practice of psychotherapy. Gwinnett Center for Counseling and Psychotherapy, 3955 Lawrenceville Highway, Lilburn, GA 30247.

© 1985 by The Haworth Press, Inc. All rights reserved.

people fear being abandoned. The majority of us find it preferable to have a mate, to have a family, or friends around at least most of the time. No one likes being rejected, being alone most of the time, being mateless, rootless, unattached, floating about in the sea of humanity like a piece of debris on the waves. For some the fear is overpowering. The search for the Other who is to serve as insurance against abandonment is intense, unrelenting. Perhaps because women define their worth and their sense of security to such a great degree through their attachments to others, women seem more likely to report this fear. Women seem more prone to experiencing the unconnected state as unbearable.

B. was a professional woman in her early 40s. She could not be without a man, no matter what kind of man, or under what conditions. For a year in therapy she had gone back and forth in her involvement with a very disturbed man, breaking up with him only to call him up in a week's time, begging him to see her again. She could manage without him during the day. She could fill up her days with work, with friends, and church, and working on an advanced degree; but she could not fill up her nights. She could not sleep without sedation, and when she slept, she dreamt horrible dreams of being lost, shipwrecked, being trapped in a burning house. And when she could not sleep, she woke up feeling empty, desperate. She would fill herself up with food, then vomit. She could not find peace in the aloneness of sleep, yet, strangely enough, she could not go to sleep with a man either. She had casual sex with numerous men, yet the involvements were superficial and did not fill up the emptiness. Several times her pursuit of the Other culminated in a massive anxiety attack in a hotel room in a distant city with a man she hardly knew. Her fears of being abandoned gave me the sensation of falling down a crevasse.

Suomi and Harlow (1972), in a study of questionable ethics, once attempted to induce depression in 45-day-old infant monkeys by separating them from their mothers and placing the baby at the bottom of an opaque box, 2 feet deep by 6 inches wide, where they remained undisturbed for 45 days. They were literally put in the "dark pit" of abandonment that humans fear they will fall into. Needless to say, the experiment was a success. The monkeys were morbidly depressed and withdrawn. When released, they would lie huddled in a corner, clasping themselves and rocking. I'm sure their desolation was infinite as they searched up the dark walls of the box for a pair of maternal primate eyes only to see perhaps the wire mesh of the tops of their cages, the light fixtures on the laboratory ceiling.

(2) Fear of having no impact. This fear is difficult to name. It has to do with being heard, being seen, being felt. It has to do with initiating some action which has an effect on the immediate environment, especially the people in one's immediate area. It is the fear of attempting to bring about a result, only to realize that one's efforts are in vain. There is no

response. And if there is no response, then one must question whether one fully exists in the world. And if one does not fully exist but exists only partially, unable to make sufficient contact with others, then one is relegated to the remotest kind of isolation from others.

R. was a very dysfunctional woman whom I saw for about 2 years. She felt at times like she was very small, so small no one really noticed her or paid any attention to her. She felt that clerks in stores would not wait on her because she was only a child, a person of no consequence. She felt that at times she could even make herself invisible. She lives in a furnished apartment, having made no changes in the place in several years' time. She drifted from city to city with a minimum of possessions. She left jobs after 6 months to a year, because it seemed that it took people about that long to notice her. She tried to be as unnoticed as possible, not to talk to anyone except through the false self she had constructed.

She had a repetitive dream in which she was on a bus, trying to get the driver's attention so that he would stop and let her out. She would open her mouth, yet nothing would come out. She would try to move but her limbs were heavy. They would move through the air as if it were a viscous liquid. Her stop was approaching nearer and nearer and she was becoming more frantic. She would struggle to scream. No one would notice her at all. She would reach toward the driver whose back was turned to her, realizing he had no awareness at all that she was even on his bus. R. was ambivalent about whether she wanted to have an impact on her environment. To not have an impact was to live in complete isolation and she was at times quite lonely. Yet to attempt to really exist in the world meant her making a full commitment to living in the world as a grown-up who both initiates and takes full responsibility for her actions. To affect others would mean that other people in turn would initiate actions toward her which might be overwhelming.

Which brings us to our next fear.

(3) Fear of being overwhelmed by a significant Other. There are individuals who fear being literally annihilated by others—not annihilated in the ordinary sense of being killed, bodily, physically, but killed off psychologically. The fear is that someone more powerful will crush their psychological apparatus. It is as if we carry about inside us a sense of our own ego boundaries which may vary from quite sturdy to very fragile. There are those who may have a conception of their psyche as being like the "black box" in a jetliner: no matter what trauma the plane may undergo, the black box will survive for some length of time. It is indestructible. Others among us feel more like eggs left abandoned in a nest. We're held together by a thin shell; inside, we are blobs of soft protoplasm, partially formed, not yet ready to endure the outside world. We can be stepped on, crushed, cracked, punctured, even eaten whole by another creature.

52 *PSYCHOTHERAPY AND THE TERRORIZED PATIENT*

Some psychotherapy patients do present the fear that they are about to be overwhelmed, devoured by, or fused into the person of another, particularly the person of the therapist. The thin membrane around their psychological apparatus offers no sense of protection. It is porous, likely to give way. D. was a woman, who, after seeing me with her husband for a year, and developing a basic level of trust in me, was able to tell me that she was, in fact, quite terrified of me. My presence in the room with her was so overwhelming, she scrutinized my every comment, gesture, and facial expression for signs of evil intent. After a year and a half in therapy, she was fascinated with the idea of touching me. She sent me articles, books, pictures, cards about touching. If I sat too close to her, I frightened her. If in the course of the hour, I made a gesture which appeared as if I was about to approach her or if I walked past her too closely, she was immobilized by fear.

She interacted quite adequately with others in her daily environment. She had constructed a "false self" for the world who was not afraid of others. The real self, however, had long ago gone underground. As a child she was victim to a schizophrenic mother who pinched, slapped, and otherwise abused her. Turning to her father for contact at age seven, after her mother had become withdrawn, her father began to sexually molest her and continued to do so for 10 years. The only early positive memory of contact with another person she could recall was a series of visits over the course of a few summers to visit an aunt. D. had been nearly psychologically annihilated most of her life. Unable to have positive contacts with her parental figures, she became "frozen with fear."

As she was becoming unfrozen in the course of therapy, she was also flooded with anxiety. She experienced a rush of loving, sexual, and aggressive impulses coming at her from others. Sometimes she wasn't sure if these feelings were coming from others or from herself. When I talked about myself, she thought I was talking about her. She had dreams in which she was holding me down, then we merged into each other and I was holding her down. She dreamt of me helping her to give birth to her daughter, of her giving birth to herself, of my giving birth to her. At times I was fused with the bad mother, or the good aunt, or the bad father. At times she was fused with me and thus with all aspects of her experience of me.

Over the months she began to consolidate her sense of boundaries. We constructed for her an imaginary "force field" around her which was flexible but impermeable and which had controls she could operate, so that she could turn it up or down as needed. As she began to feel stronger, less vulnerable, she was able to see actions, thoughts, and feelings as originating inside her. This was a new idea and a rather scary one. Which leads us to our next fear.

(4) Fear of going out of control. This name is a general one and covers

Elizabeth M. Ellis 53

many fears which may not seem very similar. This fear is not the simple everyday fear of going out of control and doing something embarrassing, venting one's anger at another, becoming overwhelmed by one's grief, and so forth. This is a darker fear of loss of boundaries, a fear of losing what civilized limits we have on our behavior and descending into madness. This fear is actually experienced as a descent, a losing one's grip, a sliding downward toward a dark chasm. It is a fear of giving up one's mental apparatus, one's processing functions, and sliding into a sea of murky, incomprehensible experiencing. It is expressed in the office as a fear of going crazy, of dying, of coming apart at the seams. It may be experienced as an implosion, a regression toward an infantile, disorganized state. Or it may be felt as an explosive movement, a flinging outward of one's body parts in all directions. A corollary of the fear of going out of control is the fear of exploding outward with such force that one destroys those upon whom one is dependent. As opposed to the fear of being overwhelmed by a significant Other, this is a fear of overwhelming a significant Other.

S. had a recurring dream about "the worm." The worm was in the basement of a dormitory in which she lived in the dream. My picture of it as she described it was something akin to Jabba the Hut in the film, *Return of the Jedi.* It was pale and viscous like a larval form of an insect. Its skin was sticky and covered with a film of dirt and debris. This worm was so huge it filled the basement and was moving up the stairs. It had already destroyed the boiler and all the plumbing. Its sides expanded and contracted as it grew larger with each wave of peristaltic movement. It was cracking the foundations of the building; it was growing to fill the entire space. Even more so, it was feeding on the building itself, ingesting the very structure of the place. The dreams were so malevolent, they frightened me as well. S. had a fear of slowly giving way to laziness, indifference, obesity, withdrawal, depression, and finally insanity. Her loss of boundaries was not a leap into self-destruction but a slow regression downward into repugnance and emotional torpor.

Some psychotherapy patients present with a fear of loss of control over themselves of such enormity that they may literally go berserk and destroy everything in their path. It has presented as a fear of destroying everything and everyone in the grocery store, or mowing down pedestrians on a crowded street with one's car. Dreams of earthquakes, fires, tornadoes, and volcanoes are always a bad sign in this regard. Luckily for us, people with this fear seldom act on it. What they do bring to the therapist is the question, "If I really let go of my feelings, will I overwhelm you? Will I destroy you? Will you establish boundaries for me? Are you strong enough to contain me?"

P. was one young woman who questioned whether she would overwhelm me. She had overwhelmed one inexperienced therapist with her numerous suicide attempts. The therapist gave up on her and referred her on to another, older therapist. There followed several hospitalizations in which P. tested every limit from physical fighting to attempting to hang herself with a light cord. The therapist contained her in the hospital, but, once she was discharged, referred her on to look for another sturdy, well-balanced therapist. P. knew she could be contained in a hospital setting yet had profound questions as to whether she had enough ego boundaries and a sturdy enough therapist to contain her on the outside. She had fantasies of strangling me, of burning my house down. At times when she was anxious, the room began to move for her, the rage would well up in her, and she would pace around the room or ask to go for a walk. Over the course of time, allowing her to find the right distance with me as well as physical containment, allowing her to huddle against me, appeared to ease her explosiveness. My being a firm, reliable, yet flexible source of supplies was crucial to her emotional development. Which brings us to our next fear.

(5) Fear of loss of environmental supports. Gravity is a part of our language. When teenagers are restricted to the home and no longer able to range far afield they say they are "grounded." Therapists use "grounded" the way they use the term "centered." It means feeling good, feeling solid and stable. We look at children's figure drawings and say, "He or she has both feet firmly on the ground. That's good. The child feels secure and confident." We talk of electricity being grounded, meaning connected to the earth and therefore neutralized, under control. We say, "Your argument is well grounded," meaning that it is fundamentally logical and reasonable.

We like having the ground beneath us. It is reassuring. But living in the world means leaving the ground little by little. And as we leave the ground or range far from home base, we must feel that the supports are there or that the supplies will be forthcoming. Or we must feel that we are taking home base with us, it is inside of us. Some individuals may stick close to home and some may break altitude records but the fear is the same. It is a sense of overwhelming panic, a fear that one's support is suddenly not there, or one's supplies have been cut off abruptly, and one is falling.

In the weeks after my father's death, I suffered from the vague dread that something had broken, not broken apart, but cracked in a very fundamental way that could not be repaired, ever. I had bought my house as my father's cancer was worsening. He knew he didn't have long to live and it gave him some contentment to lend me the money to help me get a household established. The house had a problem with water standing in the crawl space. When the rain came, the pump, intended to extract the water, instead deposited it back under the house, excavating a large hole under the sill at the front of the house. The dampness over the years had created a climate for termites who had eaten away much of the sill in the rear of the house.

The pump was rerouted, the rotted wood was replaced, but still I worried about the foundation giving way. When my father died that summer, I felt something crack apart. I had a vague fear that the foundation was cracked and soon the walls would begin to buckle also. I had dreams about finding lost chasms under the house, lost rooms, and whole groups of people down there. In those months after his death, these lines from Yeats haunted me:

> Turning and turning in the widening gyre
> The falcon cannot hear the falconer;
> Things fall apart; the center cannot hold;

The poem is called "The Second Coming" and expresses Yeats' vision of the dissolution of modern society. Joan Didion (1968) drew on Yeats' poem for her essay "Slouching toward Bethlehem." The essay developed out of a trip to the Haight-Ashbury District of San Francisco in the spring of 1967. She states in the preface to the book in which the essay appeared that she made the trip out of a felt need to come to terms with her own disorder. She had not been able to work for some months, paralyzed by the conviction that writing was an irrelevant act and that the world as she knew it no longer existed. She felt it imperative that she bring to the public awareness the evidence of atomization, the proof that things were falling apart. She writes:

> The center was not holding. It was a country of bankruptcy notices and public-auction announcements and commonplace reports of casual killings and misplaced children and abandoned homes and vandals who misspelled even the four-letter words they scrawled. It was a country in which families routinely disappeared, trailing bad checks and repossession papers. Adolescents drifted from city to torn city, sloughing off both the past and the future as snakes shed their skins, children who were never taught and would never now learn the games that had held the society together. (p. 94)

Didion is the premiere writer on the subject of angst and dissolution in American society. Living in southern California, she is, no doubt, close to her subject. She suggests that the social fragmentation and the lack of stability that is characteristic of southern-California living comes from the state of mind that one has when one is living on the San Andreas fault. At any time, the ground may give way. The very earth is shifting beneath you in that part of the country. People live there just the same, even right on the fault line, but the sense of unease and transitoriness of all things is pervasive.

(6) Fear of being unable to respond. I place this fear last because it may be actually a corollary of one of the other five. Or maybe it is perhaps the end result of one of the others, or perhaps of any one of them. This is the fear that one has gone emotionally or psychologically dead inside and is therefore unable to respond adequately to others. It is the fear that one is in actuality not a real person, not fully alive. The body works, and the mental apparatus is processing information, but the soul has retreated; perhaps it is dead altogether.

T. was an ex-con turned salesman. He told me little of his career in crime except that he had engaged in shoplifting, armed robbery, credit-card forgery, con games, and a few crimes which he said were too unspeakable to mention. He first sought help because he had a pain in his chest that would not go away. It came after his girlfriend left him. He had had many girlfriends before but he had never had a pain like this. What did it mean? He literally had no concept of normal emotions. Over the 2 years I knew him, he had a variety of emotional states which were experienced by him only as strange bodily states. We were able to construct together a way for him to understand these bodily experiences as emotions and to give names to them. Slowly he developed a vocabulary for feeling states and began to understand himself as a whole person.

T. continued to have profound doubts as to his ability to relate to people, especially to women. He wanted to feel something more than a sexual interest in a woman but he did not know how. I recall one session in which he paced around the room describing a disturbing and bizarre dream he had had. He said he had an unspeakable fear of something that he could not express. Over the course of the hour he gathered the courage to express it. He had a fear of being unable to love someone. He felt there was something missing in him. There was a vital piece of him that was not there, that had gone dead, killed off years ago. He often used the word ''dis-associate'' to describe how he would turn off his mind when things got too difficult. It had worked for him when he was unhappy as a child, when he was beaten by his father, when he was lonely as a child, when he was lonely in college, when he was confined in prison. But he did not want to dis-associate any more. He would call me from phone booths in distant cities, telling me he was about to dis-associate, and asking me to make him stay with it, to stay in touch with reality and feel whatever he was feeling and to name it.

It was only toward the end of therapy that he recalled when he first learned to dis-associate. His parents were Lithuanian immigrants and they came here on a ship at the end of the second world war. He thought he was about two at the time. He remembered crying and his father being so angry he picked up the annoying child and held him out over the edge of the ship, the waves lapping the hull. T. recalled that the look in his father's eyes was one of hatred. He wanted to kill the child. T. remembered vividly that at that point he thought he was going to die, and in his desperation, he reached around for the switch to turn himself off. He found it, he turned it, and went numb. His father finally put him down, but now that he had found the switch, he used it whenever he needed it. It was his way of surviving when he felt overwhelmed by murderous internal or external forces.

The previous list of primitive fears was made many months before I ran across the work of D. W. Winnicott. A pediatrician-turned-child psychoanalyst, Winnicott wrote prolifically in the 1940s, 1950s and early 1960s about psychological development in infancy and early childhood. In the introduction to his work by Davis and Wallbridge (1981), I ran across the following list of what Winnicott referred to as "primitive agonies" or "unthinkable anxieties":

1. Going to pieces
2. Falling forever
3. Having no relation to the body
4. Having no orientation
5. Complete isolation because of there being no means of communication. (pp. 46-47)

This list and my list are remarkably similar. Winnicott, in his studies of infants, had arrived at a set of fears that were quite like those of deeply troubled adults. Here then, we have a line of continuity from the beginning of life, and a metaphor for understanding what it is like to experience overwhelming fears. The metaphor is that of an infant, in a crib, in all its helplessness and vulnerability. Such an infant has only the barest outline of a sense of separateness from others, the most minimal control over its environment, and very little capability for self-defense.

Winnicott uses the terms "impingement" and "trauma" to elaborate his hypothesis of the origin of severe psychopathology in adults. Within the context of the mother-child unit, the infant acts on the environment out of some felt need, expressed through sound or movement. The mother responds in a way that satisfies the need, and thus contact is made with the world. Also, the mother or the environment acts upon the baby in a way that the infant must respond to. Hopefully, this impingement is one to which the infant can respond adequately. The "holding environment," meaning the mother-father-home that surrounds the infant, has as its main function the reduction of overwhelming impingements to the infant. In other words, some impingements may be too overwhelming for the infant, or occur before the infant has sufficient ego boundaries to handle them, or occur too soon on the heels of the last one and thus before the infant has recovered and prepared itself for the next one. Such impingements are referred to as trauma and result in a threat of annihilation. Examples of these impingements are those listed.

If impingements occur where support from the holding environment is

58   *PSYCHOTHERAPY AND THE TERRORIZED PATIENT*

missing, or the infant lacks competence, then primitive agony, "intense beyond description," is suffered for a split second before defenses in the ego can be organized against it. Let us hypothesize a bit about these primitive agonies, returning again to the infant in the crib. Imagine, if you will, being this infant. Suppose you are pulled from the breast abruptly and put into your crib where you are particularly hot or cold or uncomfortable. Perhaps your head is at an odd angle and you're having trouble breathing but no one comes to remedy your situation. In the darkness you feel disoriented; perhaps you begin to be hungry, but still no one comes. Many hours go by, your discomfort continues, you have a vague perception that no one will ever come. There is no one around. Thus there will be no end to your discomfort. Such must be the precursor of the fear of abandonment.

Or perhaps you cannot breathe easily, and you cry, and someone comes in the room and looks at you but does not see what the problem is. You cry again and this time you are fed instead, but you are not hungry. Or perhaps you are hungry and attempt to signal this but are given a toy instead. Or perhaps by this time, your cry is ignored by those around you as meaningless. When you do play, you smile but no one smiles back. You make sounds but no one repeats them. In other words, reactions of others to you do not have a one-to-one correspondence with your impingements on your environment. Such must be the early origins of feeling "invisible," of feeling one has no impact.

Being overwhelmed by a significant other might occur when a parent is "invasive" to the infant, such as forcing it to feed, restricting its movement severely, or partially suffocating it accidentally. However, this fear may surface as early as 5-6 months of age, a point at which we have the rudimentary beginnings of a sense of self. If the infant is impinged upon in a traumatic way at this time, it may fear regressing to an earlier state, to the undifferentiated ego mass out of which it just emerged. Or it may emerge still later in childhood, when the child is beaten repeatedly, molested, or threatened with extinction by someone whom the child has trusted. The child's reaction seems to be to "freeze," to become immobilized, or to "dis-associate."

The fear of going out of control and destroying a significant other seems most prone to appear in the third year of life, when children are experimenting with separating from parents and exerting more control over their environment. Anyone who has seen a 2-year-old go into a screaming rage has seen a child who has become temporarily psychotic. Toddlers who are allowed to disintegrate or are placated with rewards during a tantrum, must inevitably have serious problems with impulse control as adults.

Fear of loss of environmental supports may have its earliest beginnings in failure to provide purely physical supports for the infant—letting the infant's head drop back, dropping the infant. It may also have its origin in the toddler phase, that is, not being there to catch the child when he/she begins to walk, or climbs too high on a piece of furniture and falls. One expects the parent to be there, to provide supports, but the parent is not there, either through negligence or through actual loss. Early lengthy separations from a parent may convey a sense that the holding environment is not solid; it has been cracked or perhaps broken by death or divorce. The high divorce rate in this country may forecast a society in which this fear is prevalent in otherwise normal people.

This brings us to our last fear, the fear that one has gone dead inside, that one is empty. Winnicott reasons that once the infant experiences trauma, it becomes organized toward invulnerability. Differences must be expected according to the stage of emotional development of the adult or adolescent or child or baby who becomes disturbed, but what they have in common in all cases is that the individual must never again experience the unthinkable anxiety. "This unthinkable anxiety was experienced initially in a moment of failure of the environmental provision when the immature personality was at the stage of absolute dependence" (p. 49). The authors quote an axiom of Winnicott's: "Clinical fear of breakdown is the fear of a breakdown that has already been experienced. It is a fear of the original agony which caused the defense organization which the patient displays as an illness syndrome" (p. 50). Thus it may well be that T. had gone numb inside. A True Self, a core healthy ego, may have in fact retreated to some distant corner of his interior. Winnicott states that one solution to the problem, one line of defense, is to develop a False Self. In order to survive a hostile and threatening environment, the infant may develop a compliant self which is adapted to the demands of the significant others in the environment. The False Self has one positive and very important function: to hide and protect the True Self.

In his writings on trauma and the development of defenses against it, Winnicott developed a theory of the origins of psychosis and of the schizoid personality. In his later years he wrote that there was no sharp line between healthy adjustment and the schizoid experience. It seems to me that, as easily as we can respond to the metaphor of the infant in the crib, it must be that remnants of that experience remain with us. We all at times must feel abandoned or of no significance. We all experience a momentary loss of control when we fly into a rage or experience disintegration when we fall asleep or have an orgasm. Anyone who has been mugged has felt overpowered and some of the best of us have fears of falling out of the sky in airplanes. And the feeling of being detached, not quite real, is perhaps the modern malady, the burden of those who feel intensely. As T.S. Eliot's "Prufrock" says, "I go to prepare a face to meet the faces that I meet."

In an existential world, there is no holding environment. We are all as fragile and vulnerable as infants. Once we have left the holding environment of childhood, there is none to take its place. We know that we can be exposed to moments of "primitive agony intense beyond description." Hopefully, we have had good-enough-mothering and we will adapt and recover. But I wonder if the memory of the infant experience is ever completely lost.

REFERENCES

David, M., & Wallbridge, D. (1981). *Boundary and space: An introduction to the work of D. W. Winnicott.* New York: Brunner/Mazel.

Didion, J. (1968). *Slouching toward Bethlehem.* New York: Washington Square Press.

Suomi, S. J., & Harlow, H. F. (1972). Depressive behaviors in young monkeys subjected to vertical chamber confinement. *Journal of Comparative and Physiological Psychology, 80,* 11-18.

Healing the Terrorized Patient as a Model for Healing a Terrorized World

Kenneth Wapnick

INTRODUCTION

In the summer of 1984, a man walked into a McDonald's restaurant in San Diego and, for no apparent external or situational reason, began to open fire on all the customers and staff. By the time he was finished, he left 21 massacred bodies, including his own, not to mention several terrorized people who were able to escape the outward effects of his terror-crazed thinking.

In the fall of 1982, the world was horrified by what almost all people perceived to be a totally brutal massacre of scores of innocent women, children, and elderly in a Lebanese camp. The inevitable cover-ups, projections, deceptions, and the like precluded ever knowing the true cause, the agents of this cause, or the actual extent of the devastation. However, the memory of this holocaust will not be as obscured.

Jack came to therapy terrorized by thoughts that the estranged husband of his girlfriend, whom he planned to marry, was going to kill him. He reported that aside from this one fear, everything was fine in his life. After 25 years of marriage, he and his wife had mutually agreed on a divorce. All seemed set with his girlfriend and her husband, too, except insofar as Jack had these nightmarish thoughts which he could not explain.

Aside from the obvious experiences of terror, what do these three examples have in common? A closer examination of the dynamics of Jack's experience enables us to understand all experiences in which terror plays a part. Jack, who had some training and experience in counseling, sought to explain his dilemma in terms of an unresolved oedipal situation. His mother was abandoned by his father when Jack was a small child, and she would allow her son to come to bed with her. In ways that Jack could not specifically recall, his mother would sexually stimulate him and then

---

Kenneth Wapnick received his PhD in clinical psychology in 1968 from Adelphi University. He is in private practice and is president of the Foundation for "A Course in Miracles."

© 1985 by The Haworth Press, Inc. All rights reserved.

reprimand him for "playing with himself" and "being naughty." Thus, he felt that his current fears could be traced to the belief that sexual feelings toward women would inevitably be punished, and if another man were directly involved, be punished by that very man. Certainly, the dynamics here seem relatively straightforward, and on this level could not be denied.

After talking a while with Jack, however, a fuller history of his current relationship began to emerge and this seemed even more relevant to his terrorized predicament. He had known his girlfriend for about 3 years prior to his coming for therapy, when she was his housecleaner. After about a year or so, Jack began to develop romantic and sexual feelings toward her, which were reciprocated. Thus, for some time they conducted a clandestine affair, hidden from their respective spouses. Jack's guilt over this now surfaced, and it was not long before he could understand the specific connection between his terror, perceived to be rooted in his girlfriend's husband, and his guilt over his secret attacks on the unknowing man. His terror ultimately had nothing to do with the husband, but rather with his own guilty thoughts. Believing that he had attacked his lover's husband, he now believed her husband would attack him in return. Incidentally, we are not concerned here with questions of morality or "reality," but rather with Jack's own inner beliefs and perceptions. The recognition of this connection between his guilt and his terror was the beginning step in his healing. We shall return to his situation later in the article.

These three examples of terror, though different in form, share similar dynamics in terms of their experience, whether in the terror of the actual participants or that of the so-called observer. Terror's basic cause is the belief in our own terrorized inner reality which, as with Jack, becomes projected onto certain events perceived to be external to us. The belief that terror is real in the perception—that is, that its cause rests in some event or situation that is outside our mind in the physical world—justifies our reactions of horror, fear and anger. Few people in the world would find fault with such reactions, yet 50 million "Frenchmen," as our historical experience would bear out, *can* be wrong. It is the purpose of this article to suggest an alternate way of understanding the phenomena of terror, and, therefore, an alternative to dealing with such experiences. Specifically, I shall be discussing the therapeutic understanding of terror as a paradigm for understanding terror in the world.

THE WORLD OF TERROR

Our world is like an inverse funnel: What we pour through the narrow end is what comes out the larger end; the world we recognize as real within ourselves is the world we recognize as real outside ourselves. *A*

Course in Miracles (1975) puts it this way: "Projection makes perception" (text, p. 415). What we perceive inside is what we project out through the funnel of our mind and perceive outside; or, better, what we *believe* to be outside our minds.

Thus, if we perceive anything external to us as fearful, whether on a personal or international level, it can only be because we have perceived fear or terror within us. This does not deny our *perception* of these events but rather the *interpretation* we have placed upon these events. In a previous article, I discussed this shift from seeing people expressing evil to seeing people calling for the love they do not believe they deserve (Wapnick, in press). It is a shift that presents tremendous consequences for the practice of psychotherapy, not to mention for the world at large. Let us begin by examining the world of terror in which we live.

No one who walks this earth could deny that our journey here is one of fear of almost imminent annihilation or destruction, either from forces perceived as external, or from our own perceived nothingness—the suspicion that at any moment we could disappear into oblivion. From this perspective, our lives are seen as attempts to cope with this terror, making any adjustment—physical, psychological, social—that would enable us to survive without such crippling anxiety.

We seem to live in a Kafkaesque world which makes no sense except insofar as we attempt to make sensible our coping with a nonsensible world. Many psychologists would all too readily dismiss the work of Franz Kafka as the mere projection of his tortured mind. No one familiar with Kafka's journals and letters could doubt the truth of this statement. However, his popularity among those who identify with this experience of existential alienation attests that his tormented voice spoke for many voices. Almost all of us feel ourselves to be vulnerable aliens in a world that threatens us at every turn.

Gnosticism, the religious movement that reached its zenith—at least in Christendom—in the second century A.D., is enjoying a renascence now with the discovery in Egypt of a virtually intact gnostic library. Hans Jonas (1963), who has written perhaps the definitive introduction to this goldmine of a subject area, has likened the gnostic world-stance to modern-day existentialism, focusing on the perceived alienation from a world that stands apart from God, and thus apart from any inherent meaning within itself (pp. 320-340). In many moving passages the gnostics described the discomfort and even terror of being imprisoned in a world of strangeness in which they did not feel at home.

In this sense, we are all like the gnostics, sharing this same terrorized perception of our existential situation in the world. For most of us, this terror is defended against by various psychological mechanisms, of which denial and projection are the most basic. Our first line of defense is continually to repress what we really believe about ourselves. Kafka's haunting image of awakening in the morning to find one is a cockroach finds a more intellectualized counterpart, if not an equally powerful statement, in *A Course in Miracles*:

> You think you are the home of evil, darkness and sin. You think if anyone could see the truth about you he would be repelled, recoiling from you as if from a poisonous snake. You think if what is true about you were revealed to you, you would be struck with horror so intense that you would rush to death by your own hand, living on after seeing this being impossible. (Workbook, p. 159)

Once we have sought to deny what we believe is the painful truth about our self, our defensive system demands that we project this self onto others, choosing to see our own evil and sinful darkness in them, rather than in ourselves. Yet we perceive a world that our guilt has chosen that we see. Let us quote again from *A Course in Miracles,* which describes the world that the messengers of our internal fear and guilt bring back to us:

> Its messengers steal guiltily away in hungry search of guilt, for they are kept cold and starving and made very vicious by their master, who allows them to feast only upon what they return to him. No little shred of guilt escapes their hungry eyes. And in their savage search for sin they pounce on any living thing they see, and carry it screaming to their master, to be devoured. . . . They . . . bring you words of bones and skin and flesh. They have been taught to seek for the corruptible, and to return with gorges filled with things decayed and rotted. To them such things are beautiful, because they seem to allay their savage pangs of hunger. For they are frantic with pain of fear, and would avert the punishment of him who sends them forth by offering him what they hold dear. (pp. 382-383)

Indeed, our perceived world does offer us innumerable opportunities to justify such perceptions. Consider some of the witnesses it provides to support such messages from these messengers of fear. In addition to the aforementioned San Diego and Lebanese massacres, not to mention the "Final Solution" of Adolph Hitler, there are the almost daily reports of brutal rapes, murder, or incest. In recent memory there are the bizarre accounts of Jonestown and the Manson killings.

Who, truly, could deny the terror we live in? Inhabitants of large cities, not to mention many small ones, avoid terror by avoiding certain sections during certain hours, or other sections altogether. Or they attempt to shield themselves from the terror-filled world by ignoring newspapers and news programs. Yet external avoidance of terror does not undo its source in our mind. It merely enables us to avoid our fear of the outside "causes" we projected onto. Peace can result temporarily from such practices, and this is almost unavoidable in our world, but we would be mistaken to conclude that this is the peace of God.

Peace that comes from controlling the outside world is always contingent upon such controls working. We know only too well from our therapeutic experience that maintaining defenses also maintains the anxiety or fear that is underneath them. The Course states that "all defenses *do* what they would defend" (text, p. 334), teaching that as long as we invest our efforts in maintaining a defense, we are also reinforcing the fact that we *need* this defense to ward off the greater fear from within. Thus, defenses are made to "protect" us from our fear, but in truth merely reinforce its presence by teaching us that we do, in fact, need them for protection. It is an example of the vicious cycle our neurotic need for self-punishment revels in. Thus, in all such occurrences we conclude that the threat of terror is from without, rather than from ourselves. We do not realize, as in fact many of the gnostics did not, that our alienation is not because of the world but because of our mind: We are alienated from our selves, or better, from our true Self.

THE PSYCHOLOGY OF TERROR

Our patients, therefore, present very specific portraits of the terror that is within each of us, mirroring our terrorized selves as well as offering an opportunity to heal this perception of our selves. I have already discussed in more detail how our patients offer the opportunity of healing what our projection has perceived in them (Wapnick, in press). This dynamic then becomes the method, not only of bringing peace to ourselves and our patients, but for bringing peace to our terrorized world.

To understand better the actual mechanics of projection we need consider again the image of a funnel. Its narrow opening not only represents the individual mind that projects outward what it has first perceived inward, but also represents the oneness of all minds. Our perceptual apparatus continually deludes us into believing that the perceptual world—one of separation, differences, and the body—is the true and valid world. However, this perceptual experience is a gross distortion of the reality that is beyond the body and all form.

The idea of the illusory nature of the phenomenal universe, opposed to the reality of the unified world of spirit, finds interesting agreement between the mystical traditions of the world and contemporary physics. The 20th-century revolution in scientific thought rested, in part, on understanding that the Newtonian dichotomy between the inner and outer worlds, or between subject and object, was spurious: The observer cannot be separated from the observed. Many researchers in projective techniques have drawn similar conclusions. I have discussed this issue in an earlier book (Wapnick, 1983), while references that specifically address the confluence of physics and mysticism include Capra (1983), Zukav (1979), and Wilber (1984). Further discussion here would be beyond the scope of the present article.

The process of perception is similar to a prism that distorts a unified light field by breaking the light into different patterns. In truth, we are not separate minds but one mind. However, through the illusions that perception has introduced to our experience we mistakenly believe that our minds are not only separate and private, but that our true identity is found in separate bodies and personalities. It is a mistake, therefore, for therapists to believe that their thoughts and feelings have no effect on their patients; that we, as therapists, have in fact private thoughts that can be kept hidden. Minds *are* separate in the inherently unreal world of perception, but in the reality of spirit we are one, joined in the one love of God whose being we share with all creation.

What affects one mind must therefore affect all minds, just as holistic medicine has demonstrated that what affects one part of the organism— physical, psychological, or spiritual—affects all of it. The part and the whole cannot be separated and split off. The quantum physicist's holographic view of the universe reflects a similar view. The often quoted lines of John Donne are relevant here as well:

> No man is an island, entire of itself; every man is a piece of the continent, a part of the main. . . . any man's death diminishes me, because I am involved in mankind; and therefore never send to know for whom the bell tolls; it tolls for thee.

Thus, the experience of terror in San Diego, Lebanon, or in our patients ultimately comes from the terror hidden in the darkened crevices of our mind and all minds. The problem was that we did not know it was there, for we believed we had seen it elsewhere. Psychotherapy offers us the unique opportunity of remembering this truth for ourselves by teaching it to our patients.

My patients' terror is beyond my control to change, for I did not choose it for them, but it *is* within my control to change my decision to share it with them. This I can do; in fact, it is the *only* thing I can do. There is a passage in the Course that expresses this principle well. The subject is that of physical sickness, but in this quotation I have changed the verbal setting to reflect the specific context of psychotherapy for the terrorized patient:

> What must the therapist do? Can he change the patient's mind for him. Certainly not. . . . These patients do not believe they have

chosen terror. On the contrary, they believe that terror has chosen them. Nor are they open-minded on this point . . .

To them God's therapists come, to represent another choice which they had forgotten. . . . (Their) thoughts ask for the right to question what the patient has accepted as true. . . . The truth in their (therapists) minds reaches out to the truth in the minds of their patients, so that illusions are not reinforced. (Manual, p. 18)

Our terrorized behavior is a defense against the inner terror we all share as separated children of God. The terror originates in the belief that we have separated ourselves from our Creator, who is now vengefully plotting against us, threatening destruction because of what we believe we did to Him. We can observe here, incidentally, the true origin of the Freudian insight into the oedipal dilemma. Freud, as in many other instances, understood well the dynamic he was describing, yet was blind to its actual derivation and meaning.

This underlying terror, now split off from its source, becomes projected outward. Now we believe that we are afraid of what is without, or even what has been projected "inward" onto certain intrapsychic constructs such as the Freudian superego or Sullivanian "bad me." Yet all the while the true nature of our terror—our guilt over our attack on God and fear of His reprisal—remains hidden from us.

Terror, then, originates in separation, and thus it is the undoing of separation that undoes terror. This is the purpose of psychotherapy: to offer our patients the healing love of God through our forgiveness of them. We accept the fact together that our belief in having separated from our Creator has not changed the reality of our oneness with Him nor His love for us. This acceptance need not be conscious in either therapist or patient, for the decision to come together—one to ask for help, the other to offer it—is enough to fulfill God's purpose. It is not necessary, moreover, for patient *or* therapist to believe in God. God is beyond belief and He is often irrelevant to religions that bear His name or claim to represent Him. A companion pamphlet to *A Course in Miracles*, "Psychotherapy: Purpose, Process and Practice" (1976), emphasizes that it is not the forms we use that are meaningful, but their content:

Some forms of religion have nothing to do with God, and some forms of psychotherapy have nothing to do with healing. . . . (Yet) true religion heals (as) must true psychotherapy be religious. . . . To be a teacher of God (the Course's term for anyone who seeks to practice its principles), it is not necessary to be religious or even to believe in God to any recognizable extent. It is necessary, however, to teach forgiveness rather than condemnation. . . . Yet if pupil and teacher join in sharing one goal, God will enter into their relationship because He has been invited to come in. In the same way, a union of purpose between patient and therapist restores the place of God to ascendance. . . . If any two are joined, He must be there. (pp. 5-6)

In this joining, therefore, we do not make real the illusion of external causes for our distress, but rather demonstrate by our reactions that terror and conflict come from within—the decisions of our mind—and thus peace also comes from within. This is the true meaning of forgiveness.

PSYCHOTHERAPY AS THE END OF TERROR

A patient's terror, therefore, becomes the instrument of healing when we choose to see in it the reflection of our own hidden terror. Again, what we react to or judge against only mirrors what we have first judged against in ourselves. As *A Course in Miracles* states: "When you feel that you are tempted to accuse someone of sin in any form, do not allow your mind to dwell on what you think he did, for that is self-deception. Ask instead, 'Would I accuse myself of doing this?' " (Workbook, p. 243).

This congruence between inner and outer perceptions is not always on the level of form, but *is* always on the level of content or meaning. For example, we hear about a rape and feel horrified hatred for the rapist. This does not necessarily mean that we are accusing ourselves of rape in its sexual form, but it does mean that we are seeing ourselves as rapists in its more general meaning. What is rape but the psychological and/or physical overpowering of another so that our needs and desires are met without any concern for the other person? And who in this world has not at some point or another, within any given day, placed his or her personal interest above another's through domination or manipulation? Goethe insightfully recognized near the end of his life that he was guilty of every sin or crime that had ever been committed, for they had been in his thoughts at some time or another. Thus, too, do we all stand accused in our minds of the sins we perceive and condemn in others.

Therefore, we are not seeing this person sitting opposite us *as* opposite us—a patient in our office—but rather as a brother or sister walking beside us. Making another's terror real by seeing it outside of ourselves, and therefore separate from us, can only reinforce the premise of separation that underlies all terror.

This does not mean that therapists do not have a responsibility within their particular role to help alleviate another's suffering and pain, nor that they cannot employ traditional means of doing so if these indeed are helpful. Our emphasis here is on the attitude of the therapist, which must precede any verbal or physical behavior. Again, projection makes perception. The essential element, then, is not our specific interventions to undo terror, but our *perceptions* of terror. Psychotherapy, by definition if not always by practice, is the healing of the soul or mind. It reflects the change of mind about what we have made real—separation, guilt, anxiety, attack, terror—thereby looking at "reality" differently. As the Psychotherapy (1976) pamphlet states in its introduction:

> Psychotherapy is the only form of therapy there is. Since only the mind can be sick, only the mind can be healed. Only the mind is in need of healing. This does not appear to be the case, for the manifestations of this world seem real indeed. Psychotherapy is necessary so that an individual can begin to question their reality. . . . the patient must be helped to change his mind about the "reality" of illusions. . . . He must become willing to reverse his thinking, and to understand that what he thought projected its effects on him were made by his projections on the world. . . . Its (psychotherapy) whole function, in the end, is to help the patient deal with one fundamental error; the belief that anger brings him something he really wants, and that by justifying attack he is protecting himself. (pp. 1-3)

The scriptural challenge of being in the world yet not of it, which is the essential challenge of any spiritual path, is powerfully presented in just those patients who bring out in us the deeper feelings we would choose to keep hidden. This is especially so when our patients' terror becomes projected onto us, thereby causing a defensive retreat which is sometimes masked through "therapeutic interventions" that are really designed for our safety and not our patients'. Decisions to medicate, hospitalize, terminate, refer elsewhere, cancel appointments are often, though certainly not always, decisions to avoid confronting what has been brought to the surface in our own consciousness.

Thus, the pamphlet states of the patient driven even more fearful by the "threat" of healing:

> A madman will defend his own illusions because in them he sees his own salvation. Thus, he will attack the one who tries to save him from them, believing that he is attacking him. This curious circle of attack-defense is one of the most difficult problems with which the psychotherapist must deal. In fact, this is his central task; the core of psychotherapy. The therapist is seen as one who is attacking the patient's most cherished possession; his picture of himself. And since this picture has become the patient's security as he perceives it, the therapist cannot but be seen as a real source of danger, to be attacked and even killed.

The therapist, then, has a tremendous responsibility. He must

70 PSYCHOTHERAPY AND THE TERRORIZED PATIENT

meet attack without attack, and therefore without defense. It is his task to demonstrate that defenses are not necessary, and that defenselessness is strength. This must be his teaching, if his lesson is to be that sanity is safe. (pp. 9-10)

This response of defenselessness on the part of the therapist is the central healing "technique" of successful psychotherapy, just as it must be for successful efforts on behalf of peace. To believe that defensiveness—born out of fear, and its sustainer at the same time—is the means of bringing about peace is as insane as the underlying premise of separation. Beginning with an insane premise can only lead to an insane conclusion.

The world is sustained by this insane premise that attacking others—whether in deed or thought—protects us. It is part of the insane defensive system we all share, explicitly or implicitly. The San Diego killer could not have acted as he did without somehow believing he would be better off as a result of his murderous spree. The people and governments responsible for the Lebanese massacre must have believed that their best interests were being served at the expense of the inhabitants of the camp. Hitler's "Final Solution" was his personal solution for the paranoid terror he knew within. Attack is the reinforcer and sustainer of terror because our "justified" defense merely makes us guiltier: On some level we know that our attack is inherently unjustified for the other is merely the scapegoat for our own perceived sinfulness. Moreover, attack increases our fear of retaliation, which in turn justifies further defense. This is the ego's insane cycle of attack-defense, the principle underlying the nuclear-arms madness that focuses so much terror in the world.

The only true goal of psychotherapy, since it is the only means of bringing peace to the world, is the undoing of the premise that attack can protect us. We as therapists are presented with the terror radiating out from our patients, and rather than making this expression of terror real by identification or defense, we recognize that our perception of terror is the reflection of our first having made it real in our mind. Thus are we given the opportunity of seeing our own perceived terror in another, forgiving it there, and thereby forgiving it in ourselves. In this process we are no longer seeing our patients as *separate* from us but as a *part* of us, as we are part of them. The true source of the world's terror then—the belief in separation—is undone where it exists, and we are healed. The pamphlet states as the only requirement on the part of the therapist:

What must the therapist do to bring healing about? Only one thing; the same requirement salvation asks of everyone. Each one must share one goal with someone else, and in so doing lose all sense of separate interests. . . . Let him (the therapist) be still and recognize his brother's need as his and see that they are met as one, for such they are. What is religion but an aid in helping him to see that this is so? And what is psychotherapy except a help in just this same direction? (p. 6)

What does this mean for us as psychotherapists? Take the example of Jack we discussed at the beginning of the article. If we as therapists feel any guilt in ourselves for betrayal or infidelity, regardless of its form, then we shall have made Jack's terror of his girlfriend's husband real, for we must have first made it real for ourselves. Thus, regardless of our therapeutic skill and intuitive words, we would be giving our brother the underlying message that his guilt is real and the terror of retaliation justified. If, however, we are free from the vise of our projections we will, without judgment, help Jack lift himself above the battlefield he has made for himself and see his past choices that now can be corrected. His guilt can be looked at open-mindedly by both therapist and patient who have joined together at this altar of forgiveness. With guilt undone, the resultant terror is undone as well. Satisfying healing's one requirement of joining through forgiveness enables us to step aside and allow the Holy Spirit to heal through us.

THE ROLE OF THE HOLY SPIRIT

Perhaps our greatest mistake is believing that we as therapists know what is best for our patients, just as peacemakers in the world may share the similar illusion that they know what is needed to end the world's problems. This is a reflection of what Judeo-Christianity has understood to be ''original sin''—the belief we can usurp God's role and be separate from Him and His creation.

Healing occurs when we are able to set aside our own judgments of the problem or its solution, and thus be open to the Holy Spirit who will guide our words and actions. He is the aspect of God that extends into this world to correct our distorted thinking, and it is simply an extension of the original error to believe that we can correct these distortions on our own. Only He can know what is truly helpful, whether in the psychotherapist's office or in the world at large. Since all problems are the same, regardless of their form, so must their solution be the same as well. As the Course puts it: one problem; one solution (workbook, p. 141). Once we have undone our belief in separation, we have allowed God's Solution to work through us. *Passive* to our ego investment in perceiving separation, we become *active* to the unified vision of the Holy Spirit, whose guidance may in fact be as direct in its behavioral implications as is the ego's. The difference lies not in *what* we do, but *how*—through forgiveness rather than vengeance.

Therefore, we may restate psychotherapy's one requirement as setting aside the interferences to hearing the Holy Spirit more clearly, whether we know this Voice as a therapeutic hunch, listening with our third ear, or most simply, inspiration. It is our thoughts of guilt, fear, and attack that interfere with our hearing Him. Undoing these ego distortions, born of the belief in separation, comes through the forgiveness of each other that enables us to join with those whom we had heretofore seen as separate. In the context of psychotherapy, this process is enhanced by our looking beyond the seeming causes of terror to its ultimate cause of separation—within ourselves. We simply choose the miracle of forgiveness, allowing the Holy Spirit to extend it and to guide us in whatever forms of healing would be most effective.

* * *

The terror we confront in our offices is the microcosm of the terror we experience in the world—personal or international. There are not two worlds—the inner world of our mind and the world we perceive outside it—but only one. Terrorized patient, terrorized therapist; crazed assassin, terror-stricken victim—all are one, for we share thoughts of attack as one. Saint and sinner, sane and insane, are all part of the one mind that *is* this world. Therefore, changing one part of this mind changes all minds. If people choose not to accept this healing, it is held in their minds for "safekeeping" by the Holy Spirit until the time when it can be accepted. The forgiving love we extend to our patients is available to them, long after therapy has ended, whenever their choice is made. The forgiving love we extend to the world's enemies is available to them as well, perhaps long after their earthly sojourn has ended, whenever their choice is made.

Thus is peace brought to the world, whether it be the world of our office or the world at large, for they are one: "The room becomes a temple, and the street a stream of stars that brushes lightly past all sickly dreams" (Course in Miracles, 1975, p. 15). Each of us—therapist and patient alike—comes together to worship at this united altar of forgiveness, and we hear God's Voice remind us we are one in Him. Our separated stars become One Star, and to the mind that is the only locus of war, peace has come again at last.

REFERENCES

A course in miracles: Text, workbook for students, manual for teachers. (1975). Tiburon, CA: Foundation for Inner Peace.

Capra, F. (1983). *The tao of physics.* Boulder, CO: Shambhala.

Jonas, H. (1963). *The gnostic religion.* Boston: Beacon Press.

Psychotherapy: Purpose, process, practice. (1976). Tiburon, CA: Foundation for Inner Peace.

Wapnick, K. (1983). *Forgiveness and Jesus: The meeting place of "A course in miracles" and Christianity.* Crompond, NY: Foundation for "A Course in Miracles."

Wapnick, K. (in press). Forgiveness: a spiritual psychotherapy. *The psychotherapy patient.*

Wilber, K. (1984). *Quantum questions.* Boulder, CO: Shambhala.

Zukav, G. (1979). *The dancing wu li masters.* New York: Bantam.

The Terrorized Patient as Brutalized Person

James E. Dublin

Terror is fear which is intense enough to cause trembling. A terrified person is either trembling or defending organismically in order not to, and if so defending, is storing terror. A terrorized person, then, is one who has been terrified so badly or so many times that she or he has been unable adequately to tremble in order to discharge the organismically stored terror.

Take the case of a person—let's call her Jane—who has just witnessed a shoot-out between a policeman and a bank robber. She is normally terrified for only a short while. She then discharges the terror by trembling in a controlled way while talking about the incident, let's say first with a police team investigating the shooting and later with friends. During this discussion, Jane shudders, shakes her head in amazement and consternation, sighs, exclaims, and so forth. If, however, such discussing together with the accompanying bodily reactions does not adequately discharge the terror, she is terrorized.

Those persons I have seen in psychotherapy who were terrorized had been terrified so badly or so many times that they had been brutalized, in one sense of that word and sometimes in both. That is, they had been treated brutally, either by circumstances or by other persons, and in some instances, had been rendered into a brute condition, the condition of lacking the ability to reason. In such a condition, a person is both terrorized and terrified: terrorized as a state of being and terrified of remaining so.

In my experience, the kind of brutalization which leads to terrorization comes from three sources. The first is a single overwhelming incident resulting in great shock and loss, such as an accident or natural disaster. The second is a continuing parent-child relationship or other relationship which is brutalizing to the child/adolescent and from which he or she cannot escape. The third is a general energy field or atmosphere in which the person grows up and which is offensive enough to that person's sensitiveness and sensibilities to be brutalizing. These three sources of brutalization seem to result in three different manifestations of terror which are describable in terms of three kinds of ego dysfunction. The first results in severe but usually transient disruption of ego functioning; the

---

James E. Dublin received his PhD in Clinical Psychology from the University of Kentucky in 1969. He is presently in private practice in Stuart, Florida.

© 1985 by The Haworth Press, Inc. All rights reserved.

76 PSYCHOTHERAPY AND THE TERRORIZED PATIENT

second in severe and continuing failure of ego adaptation, often seen as psychosis; and the third in character armoring and characterological compensation that manifests as a much less severe but continuing problem of ego resiliency that shows up in the form of cognitive-interpersonal deficits. As examples, I show you now Ricardo, Mitchiko, and Jerry.

The Fates who collect, combine, and distribute musical genes smiled on Ricardo. He grew up poor but fairly treated and, because he was a musical prodigy, fairly sheltered from the knocks of life. *El afficianado niño,* his father proudly dubbed him in the *plaza,* contributing to Ricardo's winning script. Though he was born and grew up in a village in the foothills of the Andes, his reputation spread as if riding the wind, and by the time he was nine, several teachers, including Segovia himself, were courting him.

Twenty-seven he is now, a classical guitarist and composer; handsome, animated, purposeful . . . and lucky. Several albums are starting to sell now, and a solidly booked tour is in place. It's Los Angeles tonight, and 15 minutes before the curtain rises. Having done his usual prepreformance meditation, he's ready and relaxed, caressing and fondling his intimate companion, the rich-noted Alvarez given to him by his teacher 12 years ago when his hands had first reached full size. Knock on the dressing room door. Telegram. Ricardo scans its three scanty lines . . . .

> [I interrupt this scene in order to give an orientation too important to put in a footnote. My perspective is that of the "lived-body," the subjective, experiencing, living body as opposed to the body-as-object, the had body. From that perspective, body-mind-spirit is a unity but for purposes of showing that it can be phenomenologically analyzed as three-fold. From that perspective, a person is heir to shocks of the flesh and/or mind, and if either is severe enough or enduring enough, also to the spirit, the energy. We will see, in a moment, a shock to the mind-body of Ricardo, one so severe that it will grip both his muscles and his spirit as energy. In order to illustrate this threefold unity, I now write in phenomenological slow motion, so that you can see, frame-by-frame, what happens.]

. . . . The color drains from Ricardo's face, leaving it a chalky contrast to his rich purple shirt and shining black hair. His eyes widen, squint shut against the picture, blink, and open quite wide . . . to stay that way. His chest freezes, his breathing tract being reduced to a short strip in the abdomen, which begins rapid pulsations. Nausea floods him, and his abdominal, diaphragmatic, and esophageal muscles grip tight to preclude vomiting. His chin and lower lip quiver now, unleashing hard-won control and composure, and his hands begin to tremble. An ear-piercing shriek forms in the depths of him, in his *hara,* and his right hand instantly clutches there, between his navel and genitals, even while the muscles of his chest and throat lock tighter to hold the scream in. A vein running up his forehead becomes sharply erect, then flattens out, leaving him with a pale, ashen, almost-blue countenance as his heart temporarily dysfunctions. Dizzy, he stumbles to a nearby chair and sinks onto it, his hands now in a high-frequency hum, his lower jaw still quivering, his teeth chattering together. Now muscles in front of his ears and beneath them on his neck clench, and his jaw is stilled. His eyes fall on the guitar, which has fallen to the carpet near his feet, and a fantasy flashes behind his frozen-up eyelids, a fantasy of grabbing the guitar and smashing every object in the small dressing room. His adductor muscles clench, holding his legs squeezed tightly together at the knees. His trapezius muscles, running the length of his back, freeze, as do his deltoids and pectorals; all four limbs are now solidified. Finally, his scalene muscles, those that connect the back of his skull to his neck-shoulders, contract into thin sticks, holding his head level and straight ahead; and thus he sits.

Ricardo has given his last performance for a long while. He will be whisked to a nearby hospital, and with little delay, to a psychiatric facility. He will become a clinical enigma for almost 2 months, for that much time will pass before he speaks. His slightly cataleptic bodily deportment will last even longer, and it will be close to a year before he will play again, even in private.

As you have probably guessed, all that was in the telegram was a report of a divine tantrum. His quiet, sunny, flower-laden village in Peru is no more; a 17-second, 7-Richter tremor had its epicenter there. Father, mother, brothers, sisters, buddies, uncles and aunts, teachers, priests, butchers, bakers, and indeed, candlestick makers, are all at once all gone. Ricardo is alone and without hope of ever being otherwise; abandoned, empty, helpless, frozen.

On the chart they have written, "Post-Traumatic Stress Syndrome, Chronic." That is psychiatric/psychological long-hand for two words which would have said it better, "Transiently Terrorized." If I were writing a truly descriptive report on this consultation, I would describe the etiology as "Brutalized—by nature, God, luck—however you spell an earthquake propitious and circumspect enough to leave only him."

Ricardo's terror, his organismically stored trembling, will contain a rich mixture of impotence, rage, and guilt. He should have been released from the hospital much before now. They have unwittingly brutalized him further, by separating him from his guitar and by injecting him with various chemicals. If I can arrange to see him in therapy, I will want to see him at least twice a week, maybe more often at first, and I will love the hell out of him, and when he makes contact, I will tell him nothing but the truth, that I would swap places with him to be able to play guitar like he did and can again. And when he begins to stir, I will help him express his necessary trembling, verbally and bodily. How I will do that verbally is probably obvious, by listening compassionately, directing him again and again back to the areas of avoidance until he speaks of his experience and catastrophic expectations in such a way that I can hear him in his words, and when he hits that place of describing his emptiness and aloneness, I will act as a supportive reality agent. How I will do that bodily will depend on the gestalt of his blocked trembling, how it is linked associatively and bodily to other bioenergy blockages, constrictions, compensations, and to disruption of emotional flow. An inherent part of being a good musician is to feel, tolerate and identify with vibrations, and when they are right and pleasing, to tremble in excitement. Ricardo will need to be first emptied out, then retrained to tolerance of and excitement at trembling, and he then will have good-byes to say and mourning to do. He will then again have full access to the full range of his feelings and thoughts, and to his creativity. What he does or does not do then will no longer be a clinical matter but rather an existential choice. As every devotee of Tchaikovsky knows, much haunting, beautiful music comes from existential despair.

Mitchiko's was a much more common brutalization. She was a bright, bouncey, long-haired, slightly moon-faced little girl of five who loved birds, crickets, rainbows, butterflies . . . and mommy and daddy. Mommy, formerly a Yokohama hooker, wanted more than all else to get to the Mecca she knew as the United States. To get here, she married a drunken, sociopathic sailor named Harry and called Harrysan.

It was April, and they were all three in the living room of the tiny, bleak apartment near the switching tracks in Roanoke, where Harrysan worked. Watching TV they were, and Harrysan seeming no more drunk than usual, Mitchiko snuggled up to him. She disturbed him . . . or something on the evening news did . . . or something from his childhood. He grabbed her by her long hair, lifting her by it from the floor, tufts of hair-roots pulling loose under her weight, blood streaming down between her wide-open, glazed-over eyes. Once, twice, three times he struck her across the face and throat, then tossed the bleeding, screaming little Mitchiko into her mother's arms and stalked out to the nearest tavern. Mommy, having long ago cracked up and split off, consoled Mitchiko. "There, there, little one. That wasn't your father. That was the spirit of Chet Huntley."

That was 13 years ago, and Mitchiko suffered similar dehumanizing objectification from both parents—violence from father and schizophrenogenic rejection from mother—until she could flee, at age 14. Now, she's 18, and someone has found her; some social agency has brought her in. Associations tangential to bizarre. Affect volatile, blunted to agitated. Ambivalence moderate. Oriented as to place and time, at times questionably as to person and circumstances. Addicted to heroin and other substances. Malnourished. "Amenable to therapy after initial withdrawal and medical treatment?" they want to know. They've written three diagnoses, with a question about the third: (1) Mixed Substance Abuse, Continuous; (2) Childhood Onset Pervasive Developmental Disorder; (3) Rule Out Schizo-Affective Schizophrenia.

These words must all be removed from Mitchiko's world, I explain to the young social worker. The appropriate words are "brutally terrorized," I tell her. Yes, I will see her, if the agency can arrange it. Therapy will take probably a year. Mitchiko will have to be given loving structure; her ego functioning will have to be reformed, her self-esteem restored, and her worth and value as a human being and her attractiveness as a young woman made clear to her. If mommy and Harrysan try to get in the act, or either one of them individually, I will have no truck with it and will move with all the psychological-legal force I can muster to prevent their ever even seeing Mitchiko again, so if that problem comes up, I'll need her guarantee of agency cooperation. Harrysan is dead, she assures me, and Mitchiko's mother has vanished, probably back to relatives in Japan. She agrees to make the arrangements for me to see Mitchiko, and seems relieved.

Therapy took 7 months. For the first two, Mitchiko was sullen, distrustful, withdrawn. I said very little, and simply brought to each session a part of her fragmented self—a butterfly book, a rainbow window sticker, a cricket, or a lollipop. When Mitchiko was agitated, I brought music or flowers, and once we burned incense. I reminded her to re-mind herself, showing her the world that was already in her DNA—meditating, bubble baths, caressing a kitten, arranging stones and foliage together, hopscotch, tag, and boardwalk-park place. When she kissed me on the cheek and I could feel her slight trembling, I held her as tenderly as I ever have my own daughter, and she exploded into a quivering hurt that lasted through 2 weeks of crying.

After Mitchiko's initial discharge, her affect and associative process were so improved that I told the social worker to step up her efforts in finding adoptive parents, and to try for orientals or a mixed couple. While she was busy doing that, I was busy telling Mitchiko what a beautiful person she was, and since it was the truth, my job wasn't hard. She tried to prove me wrong by stealing a silk-screen from my office. I gave her a plastic Jesus and a very valuable granite Buddha, and smiled at her for an hour. She returned the silk-screen, along with a stolen Parker pen. I held her hand all the way to the store to return it, and the proprietor, picking up her energy, gave her a drawing set and some parchment paper.

During the first 4 months, she occasionally talked crazy, and when she did, I showed her how to really do that, which frightened her. Each time she trembled, I did too, in excitement, and explained the difference to her. I don't think she ever understood that, but you can't have everything, which I also explained to her.

When we were 6 months into therapy, and after the social worker had very luckily found almost ideal parents, we had to intensify our efforts, for they were getting set to move to California and understandably wanted to take her with them. We had about 12 sessions with Mitchiko, her new stepbrother-to-be, Eric, and her new parents participating. I coached them all in how to relate to Mitchiko, by simply showing them and by talking a little about ego functioning and recovery from brutalization.

Mitchiko and I had one last session together alone. She wanted to know what we had done together. I told her she wouldn't understand if I tried to tell her. In a surprising and pleasing show of spunk, she said, "try me." I said, "We ruled out schizo-affective schizophrenia by ruling trembling back in." Her brain didn't understand but her eyes did. After just a second of dull terror, they brightened as she kissed me on the cheek and said, "Thank you, Doctor Jimsan." She was trembling slightly and, unsurprisingly, there was some fear in her energy, but mostly excitement.

Jerry is a characterologically terrorized person who was brutalized over a long period of time and by degrees, by growing up in an environment in which he did not and could not fit. Never physically brutalized, he was constitutionally unsuited to his childhood and adolescent circumstances, too bright, too sensitive, and too creative to fit into the rough-and-ready, culturally and intellectually barren, tobacco-growing Tennessee energy in which fate placed him. His characterological bottom line is that he grew up in a bind, in a fear-filled energy field in which he was obliged to be or pretend to be *machismo.* He was prohibited from discharging his terror by trembling, being taught to hurry up and grow up, which in his milieu, consisted of becoming stoic, taciturn, steadfast, upright, the very antithesis of trembling.

When Jerry was four, his father, a minister with poetic aspirations, and who doted on Jerry and spent much good, loving time with him, was killed accidentally. His mother, virtually collapsing, took him to live with her parents. They were not only poverty-ridden farm folks, but since mother was the next to eldest in a long sibline most of whom were still at home, this meant living in a crowded, spartan, rigid, fundamentalistic household. Mother's family were all blessed by high native intelligence, but were all uneducated beyond grade school, and were primitive, Germanic earth-peasants. During the 72-hour work week, everybody was slightly terrified of not being able to scratch sustenance out of the 85-acre farm. And on Sundays, rather than resting, they worshiped, which consisted of working themselves into a frenzy of God-terror, which seemed to serve to propel them through another 72-hour work week so that the whole thing could be repeated endlessly.

In this subculture, boys were supposed to like whittling, fishing, collecting rocks and frogs, teasing girls, and staying dirty; but Jerry liked staying clean, and liked to draw, color, write, spell, read, cut and paste, listen to music, and to ask questions. Mother loved Jerry immensely, but without the help of a husband on whom she had been very dependent, she experienced him most basically as a burdensome mouth to feed and body to clothe. She was perceptive enough to recognize Jerry's uniqueness, but being informationally unequipped to relate to it, could not help him channel it. She spent much time trying to relate to Jerry's very bright head with her own unsophisticated one, and could never quite grasp his cognitive grasp, which was always several years ahead of his physical and social maturity. For example, after he had initially cried and whined about his father's disappearance (he was kept from seeing the mangled body), he wanted to know where he had gone. Mother and grandmother told him that father had gone "up to Heaven." When he asked where that was, they told him it was "up behind the sky," and when he wanted to know why father had gone there, they told him it was "God's will." When he wanted to know what that meant, they told him that father had died because God, for reasons which were "not ours to know," wanted him with Him.

This explanation made Jerry very angry with and frightened of an invisible being. For over a year afterward, when a nut would fall from a tree near him, he would tremble and wonder whether God was warning him, if so about what, and especially, whether God was going to take him (he half wished) to be with father and Him. It was then, at age five, that Jerry started squeezing terror into his neck and shoulders, drawing his head down into himself and forward, vigilantly protecting himself from a blow or surprise from above, laying the characterological foundation for later tendencies to obsessiveness and paranoid ideation.

It was doubly unfortunate for Jerry that his family had somehow established age nine as the cutoff point for allowing the expression of fear in male children, for it was when he was almost ten that mother's father, "Papa," as he was called, began to really lose it. Papa had been thrown from horseback and had injured his back years earlier, when he was about 40, and being opposed to all but "rubbin' doctors" (chiropractors), he never got adequate treatment. Perhaps triggered by the injury, as his family all said, and certainly in interaction with a good deal of stress as a result of being no longer able-bodied, Papa developed a progressive central nervous system disorder symptomatically resembling a combination of Huntington's chorea and Gilles de la Tourette Syndrome, and labeled by the family as "St. Vitus Dance." His arms flailed spasmodically, his shoulders jerked, his head twisted from side to side, and eventually, streams of curse words, expletives, and peculiar sounds poured from his mouth. These were never aimed at Jerry, of whom Papa was inexplicably fond, but they flew all around him, along with an occasional chair flung at someone else, until they finally had Papa carted off to the local State Mental Facility.

The additional 4 years of fear had added considerably to Jerry's characterological terror. By now, age 13, he had squeezed his buttocks' muscles in tightly and contracted his adductor and soleius muscles. Now, afraid of not being able to perform sexually should the opportunity arise, Jerry's interpersonal-social difficulties began to manifest. A year younger than many of his classmates because of fast promotion, he was unable to excel in athletics and felt quite inferior, but feigned superiority by being verbally facile and witty. Academically he excelled, and since the brighter girls liked him, he did not suffer for dates, but his inability to establish an intense buddy relationship added to his feelings of insecurity. Muscularly, he completed the picture of his fear by drawing his pelvis back, by contracting his psoas muscles. Thus he went through high school, college, and into the mainstream of life—which brings us to his first divorce, the occasion of his making clinical contact with me, about 10 years ago. Jerry has had two goes at therapy, the first for as long as I usually see anyone continually (2 years); the second more recently, following his second divorce, just drew to a close, and so I will talk about therapy with him in the present tense.

Jerry was supposed to be either an artist or a musician. He draws, paints and sculpts well, and has a fine sense of color, light, movement and perspective. His best artwork reminds me of one period of Picasso and is also not unlike some of the work of Miro. He also plays trumpet almost as well as Maynard Ferguson and on a par with Chuck Mangione or Doc Severenson. However, he will be neither an artist nor a musician, and insists on being a computer expert. And expert he is, able to design them, analyze their capacities, develop new uses for them, build them small enough to set on a thumbnail and run some major project, and even to fix them quicker than almost anyone, minimizing "down time." And in an important, debilitating way, he *is* a computer. He's very obsessive, very in the head, very cut off from feelings, which if intense, tend to terrify him, especially if they come on suddenly or involve the heart or genital functions.

Jerry's characterological terror is threefold: of abandonment, of loving, and of intense feelings. Having become psychologically sophisticated through the years, he no longer fears a god-behind-the-sky and is no longer unable to tremble as a result of being trained in stoic warriorhood. Now, at 37, he is afraid to tremble in excitement, for fear of utter loss of control, of fragmentation, explosion into bits. His normal-under-the-circumstances, slightly paranoid cognitive style has necessitated passive, avoidant control. His terror of abandonment and of being loving and interrelated manifest more in his relationships with women than with men. Though he cognitively knows better, he knows affectively that if he gets too close to a woman, she will be taken away. He is not typically paranoid, and thus is not into controlling others while perceptually manufacturing their attempts to control him. He is simply afraid that with too much contact he will both be left and torn apart, broken up. Self-protectively, he wants to remain as apart as necessary until and unless he seeks contact. This makes it nearly impossible for any woman who is not all-giving and utterly tolerant and compassionate to maintain a relationship with him. He expected both wives, who were both busy, working, career-oriented women, to cater to his peculiar contactful-contactless cycles. And they tried, but eventually could not.

Jerry's terror of intense feelings manifests also in his sexual life. After we had done enough work on his muscular-armor systems to loosen him, he began to experience orgasm as described by Wilhelm Reich in the genitally mature character: genitals-to-toes-to-head-to-toes-again ejaculatory sensations followed by strong, extended involuntary pelvic movements in turn followed by very intense feelings of ego-unity, blending, absence of separateness and apartness. This increased his terror of fragmentation-explosion and his terror of abandonment, and he further removed himself from contact with his second wife, a very sexual and fully orgasmic woman who wanted sex at least three times a week. This was too dangerous, he felt, while verbalizing delight. She would go away, he felt, and she did, but for her own reasons, being no longer able to tolerate his separate organismic sleep-work-relate cycles.

Each case of characterological terror is individual, and each person must be treated individualistically. Jerry is interpersonally schizoid, intrapsychically obsessive, cognitively a bit paranoid, characterologically oral, and bioenergetically a top-bottom energy split and character split. He is top-heavy, cognitively and physically, both his head and mind being too big to be properly synchronized with the rest of him. His buttocks are small and squeezed together, and his feet are off the ground occupationally, symbolically, and literally (poor bioenergy flow to lower legs and feet). He is primarily a deflector rather than the projector he might be with his paranoid fringe or the introjector he could be with his oppressive background and obsessive, try-hard scripting. This means that therapy has to keep on getting his attention, awakening him, then waking him again and again. He must not be allowed to space out, trip out, or "schitz" out, so therapy must be demanding, but through the personal presence of the therapist rather than as a therapy system. The terrorized person who has been brutalized cannot or will not tolerate therapy that is delivered as a system, something being done to him or her.

I had to become Jerry's friend, and I did. As an avoidance of really experiencing, he decided to learn Gestalt therapy as a system, by participating in and watching me work in groups. I allowed and encouraged this, and when he got the hang of it, he in effect co-led two weekend groups. He thus discovered he was too needy, too young, too desperate to become a good therapist. This enabled him to break through his major tendency to avoid contact with me, so that I was no longer so hard-pressed to operate purely humanistically. We entered into a program of body work. Following a lot of breathing stool-work, his hinged chest broke loose, his heart *chakra* opened somewhat, and he began to be able to experience, for the first time in a long time, his abdominal area and belly sensations, which inspired him to get back into playing the trumpet, which in turn helped with the deepening-breathing project. We worked on ownership of his eyes, freeing his chest to breathe, restructuring his shoulders and neck so that he was more or less lined up spinally and much less sloped and drooped, and we worked on his grounding with bioenergetic and Feldenkrais exercises. Eventually, he trembled, then shuddered in utter terror intermittently over a period of about 2 months, following which he cried long and hard, but dryly, deep into his center. He cried about most of the things he was certainly entitled by his background to cry about: father's and mother's abandonment of him and their ineptness; mothers' and grandmother's exhaustion; Papa's misfortune; not having had access to a decent library or a decent art teacher.

I wish Jerry had cried bitter and salty tears from childhood and hot, rageful tears from the now of having lost two wives, but he didn't. I also wish he had got into artistic/musical pursuits where his genetic gifts lay, but he didn't. He did marry a third time, to a psychic or ''psychic,'' and moved to Silicon Valley where, I understand, the computer action really is. When I spoke to him on the phone, not long ago, he was enjoying being a father, which in itself is a major transformation for him, and he sounded good.

The therapy of terror is a contact sport, but the contact must be caring, loving, as a friend. This kind of contact will evoke contactful trembling, in excitement, in orgasm, in anticipation, in joy, and in terror as a situationally appropriate response. Tremble-ability and tremble-response-ability as tremulousness will be restored. The terrorized patient must be kept in contact with his or her avoidance of excitement when in the phobic layer until implosion and trembling explosion occurs, not once but repeatedly, until the basic organismic resiliency is restored. The therapist who is acquainted with the character-muscular approach has an advantage because he or she can work externally as well as interiorly with the parts of the lived-body which have become structurally and functionally frozen.

The best therapy system (e.g., Gestalt, Bioenergetics, neo-Reichian, Rational Emotive Therapy, Transactional Analysis, etc.) to use very explicitly with a terrorized patient is none. The terrorized patient, particularly, must be treated as any compassionate person would treat a brutalized person.

We are all terrorized, to some extent. I, for example, certainly am. I would not bet that we will get to 1989 without a nuclear holocaust, if a polar flip-flop does not fling us into space before then. Meanwhile, this is what I have learned so far about working with the terrorized person.

Integrating the Splits in Crime Victims' Self Images: Toward the Reparation of the Damaged Self

Sharon Hymer

Most crime victims experience a severe assault on the self. The "invisible wounds" (Bard & Sangrey, 1979) wrought by the unexpected, traumatic nature of the crime result in damage to the victim's self-image that may take the form of diminished self-esteem, excessive use of non-adaptive defenses or exacerbation of self pathology.

This paper concerns itself with an especially prevalent vicissitude of the self that occurs following victimization—the phenomenon of splitting. Splitting was first described by Freud (1927/1961) as a defense to accommodate the ego to a traumatic reality by simultaneously acknowledging and disavowing the event. Klein (1953) then applied the concept of splitting to early object relationships in which the infant compartmentalized the object into the "all good" and "all bad" breast.

Splits occur not only between the self and object, but also between different aspects of the self. Grotstein (1981) views splitting as a universal phenomenon that "originates from the experience of existing in separate subselves or separate personalities which have never been totally unified into a single oneness. 'At-one-ment' is not only the goal of analysis; it is also the goal of life" (p. 18).

The crime victim can again become integrated—that is, approximate being at-one with the self and with others—if he or she is able to acknowledge and work through the vulnerable aspects of self and thereby integrate these components into the self totality. The victim must come to terms with the "unfinished business" (Perls et al., 1951) triggered by the victimization in order for the self to be effectively repaired.

The splits in self-image that many victims undergo can be conceptualized as taking place on three levels: (1) unconscious self-images and con-

---

Sharon Hymer, PhD, is a psychologist in private practice in New York City as well as serving as adjunct assistant professor at New York University. She is currently a member of the American Psychological Association Task Force on the Victims of Crime and Violence. Dr. Hymer has published numerous articles on a variety of topics.

© 1985 by The Haworth Press, Inc. All rights reserved.

87

scious self-images which concur with either (2) traditional societal or (3) *zeitgeist* values. Traditional social values involve long-standing societal values primarily filtered through the parents to the child, resulting in superego formation. Research findings from a variety of sources (Bard & Sangrey, 1979; Drapkin & Viano, 1974; Symonds, 1980) attest to the fact that many victims tend to internalize traditional societal views about victimization that are often stigmatizing in nature.

The zeitgeist level consists of current socio-cultural, political, or educational movements and ideologies that have not yet been fully converted into mainstream societal institutions. Zeitgeist values, such as feminism, are ideologies-in-transition. Feminist-based community-oriented victims' services involved in multiple aspects of reparation to the damaged self (e.g., teaching self-defense, providing shelters, boosting morale) constitute a prime example of the zeitgeist level as it affects victims.

Two clinical vignettes are presented to illustrate how victims struggle to integrate the splits between the unconscious and conscious self-images to achieve a more satisfactory cohesive self. In examining the splits that take place between these levels, the therapist can discern how the victim's unconscious fantasies about the self and others conflict with the social feedback (traditional or zeitgeist) received from others. The victim can then begin to reparatively acknowledge these disowned aspects of self and thereby to gradually achieve a more integrated self-image.

SPLITTING

Splitting is a universal phenomenon that occurs throughout life both between the self and others and within the self. Grotstein (1981) defines splitting as "the activity by which the ego discerns differences within the self and its objects, or between itself and objects" (p. 3).

Splitting may serve as a defense utilized by crime victims to maintain a sense of equilibrium following the trauma. Certain crime victims split off the vulnerable self that experienced the victimization from the conscious "invulnerable" self that joins with others in the victim's social circle in denying or minimizing the toll on the self triggered by the victimization.

In silently colluding with others in this manner, the victim is rendered invisible (Reiff, 1979). While the split-off vulnerable self is not acknowledged, it nonetheless often reappears in the form of symptoms characterizing the post-traumatic stress disorder (Horowitz, 1976). Nightmares, phobias, obsessions, insomnia, physiological reactions of discomfort and so on, serve as a signal to the victim that the vulnerable split-off self is still active and must be therapeutically integrated into a cohesive self system.

Another type of split within the self occurs in victims in which the traumatized self gains ascendancy. This circumstance is more likely to occur in victims in which severe self pathology has been heretofore successfully defended against to some extent. The victimization incident triggers the eruption of the problematic pathological self which, though always present, was previously regulated and better able to adapt to societal norms.

The paranoid victim, for example, employs the crime incident as an ultimate confirmation of his or her distrust of an unsafe, "evil world." As such, the previously established reasonable false self (Winnicott, 1960) that learned to navigate more or less successfully in the world is eroded by the paranoid self that has now again become the dominant component of the victim's personality.

The masochistic victim who may have made progress in altering his or her habitual self-destructive stance in the world likewise often views the victimization as external validation of the correctness of a self-punitive *weltanschauung*. This victim is able to utilize the crime incident as further evidence to add to the arsenal of self-blame (Bulman & Wortman, 1977; Janoff-Bulman, 1979). Thus, the masochistic self may again emerge triumphant with the nonmasochistic self being split off, so that this victim can attribute all negative life circumstances to the self and so justify the masochistic position.

Gestalt therapy provides another clinically useful perspective on splitting. The word *gestalt* itself refers to a meaningful, organized whole (Perls et al., 1951; Perls, 1969). This form of therapy emphasizes the unity of mind and body and encourages the recognition of bodily processes, thoughts, and emotions that have been split off from awareness. The goal of therapy is to become aware of one's total self and environment.

"Taking care of unfinished business" involves the working through of unresolved conflicts. The unfinished business of being a crime victim must be worked through so that the victim does not carry this trauma into every new relationship where the victimization may be reenacted.

Perls et al. (1951) maintain that "The average person, having been raised in an atmosphere full of splits, has lost his Wholeness, his Integrity " (p.viii). Crime victims who experience severe trauma may intensify splitting processes, either as a defense to negate, minimize, or obfuscate the crisis that the self has undergone, or, in the case of paranoid and masochistic victim types, to strengthen these entrenched aspects of self at the expense of progress gained in the direction of a strengthened nonparanoid or nonmasochistic self.

THE THREE PRIMARY LEVELS

Unconscious Level

Splits can occur not only within the self, but also between the self and others. Krupnick (1980) asserts that victims' discomfort over vulnerability is often based on a split-off unconscious expectation of personal omnipotence or total control. The negative self-image that ensues thereby results from the perception of the self's or other's failure to prevent the crime from ever having happened.

The victim who harbors the unconscious fantasy that he or she will always be protected from harm by parental figures will now see others as unreliable caretakers and experience narcissistic rage at being abandoned. Lister (1982) has found the opposite reaction in the victim who may experience intimacy with the victimizer either by way of identification with the aggressor or through gratitude for being spared. In such instances, the perpetrator is experienced as an earlier split-off parental figure who exercises life-and-death power over the victim.

For many victims, the crime incident serves to reevoke earlier repressed memories of feelings of terror, powerlessness, and anger at being a helpless child unable to deal with the frustrations inherent in many perceived unfair circumstances. The return of these repressed aspects of self now give the victim an opportunity to reparatively consolidate the self in learning to cope with the victimization and actively seeking therapy and/or prosecution to enhance self-esteem.

Bem and Bem (1970) elaborate on the impact of broader social forces on the unconscious level. They put forth the concept of a nonconscious ideology that is implicitly accepted but remains outside of awareness. If the victim and others believe that child abuse is a symptom of a sick society, for example, the belief can then be fostered that little can be done about it. Tacit acceptance of such an ideology can thereby reinforce a previously internalized powerless self-image developed during the early years.

Traditional Societal Level

Dominant societal voices reflected by the victim's family and friends often contribute to the "second injury" (Symonds, 1980) that involves the escalation in victimization as supports and the larger community further blame the victim. Lerner and Miller (1978) note many conditions in which the victim is derogated; Reiff (1979) speaks of the invisible victim that society chooses to ignore since the victimization is viewed as part of the victim's life-style or bad luck; and Bard and Sangrey (1979) describe the "victims as losers" belief syndrome. Many victims are summarily stigmatized and altogether avoided, so that others do not have to risk the danger of "contagion" (Weis & Weis, 1975).

The victim may thereby perceive himself or herself as a non-person who may either split off feelings and thoughts associated with the traumatized self or attempt to repair the self by choosing to express his or her feelings at the risk of the second injury from others.

Bulman and Wortman (1977) found that in their sample of quadraplegics and paraplegics, many victims believed that they could have avoided the accident, resulting in feelings of self-blame. In such instances of self-blame in which irrevocable physical damage has accrued to the victim, self-esteem may drastically diminish or be entirely split off from a damaged self-image that is continually being bombarded not only by negative societal feedback but also by unrelenting self-criticism.

Fattah (1979) cites two categories of victims in which societal stereotypes are particularly damaging to the self image: (1) the culpable victim in which social supports maintain that the victim had himself or herself to blame, and (2) the culturally legitimate victim constituting primarily women, lower class individuals and racial minorities who, through socialization and in connection with their marginality, come to be established as legitimate objects for victimization. Thus, in instances of wife and child beating, the notion of the family being sacred may serve to legitimize lack of police interference.

In both types of victims, the prevalence of feelings of powerlessness and disillusionment may result in the splitting off of problem-solving and coping ego functions as the helpless, often regressed self-image comes to occupy the foreground of experience.

Alternatively, Cobb (1976), Kutash (1978), and Bard and Sangrey (1979) have shown that societal support can maintain, enhance and/or repair the victim's damaged self-image. Friedman et al. (1982) reported that the more supporters victims had, the sooner they got over the post-traumatic stress of victimization. Social support is a crucial factor affecting victims' ability to cope as well as to regain ego strength and repair self-esteem. If the victim feels cared for and esteemed, he or she is better able to face the split-off thoughts and feelings that emerge in the weeks and months following the victimization and to work through the conflicts in a supportive, therapeutic setting.

Zeitgeist Level

Feminist ideology and community programs, most notably rape-crisis centers and battered-women's shelters, have had a considerable effect on the self-image of victims. Kappel and Leuteritz (1980) note some of the basic feminist ideological and therapeutic positions regarding victims. These include: viewing rape and marital abuse as a collective, structured aspect of social relations rather than an individual problem and eliminating hierarchies (e.g., among women in shelters) to get rid of unequal power distributions. The aftereffects of being a victim are attributed to social conditions rather than to psychological factors within the victim.

Maracek and Kravetz (1977) specify three central areas in which feminist therapy has concentrated:

1. Formulating corrective theories of women's psychological disorders. Being a victim would here be considered to be intrinsic to the social relations in a patriarchal culture. While the self-image of the crime victim is often suffused with self-blame, the shift in focus from self-blame to collective societal responsibility enables the victim to regain self-esteem in integrating the split-off assertive self into the prevailing self-image.
2. Providing feminist counseling and therapy. The victim who seeks help from a feminist therapist or feminist milieu in the form of a shelter is exposed to a nonhierarchical setting in which competency and self-nurturance are encouraged. As such, the victim's positive feelings about self that may have been recently split off as a result of the victimization or submerged for years in an abusive marriage are given an opportunity to reemerge and to be reparatively integrated into a more consolidated self-image.
3. Fostering women's self-help groups. In lieu of the employment of professionals that would create a hierarchy, the self-help group is based on the egalitarian principle of all women in the group being peers. The victim's self-image that is often further battered by parental figures and other representatives of traditional concerns is now able to begin a process of reparation in a supportive milieu in which both the damaged self and the split-off robust self are able to be acknowledged and worked through in order for the victim to achieve an integrated self-image.

Walker (1980) summarizes, "The theoretical orientation most clearly associated with the feminist political stance is that all violence is a reflection of unequal power relations. . . . Thus, power is seen to be at the root of all violence" (p. 344). The goal of therapy then becomes the development of autonomous, competent, self-actualized individuals—a goal that is often undermined by the development during the childhood years of a self-image congruent with the traits of passivity, compliance, and submission promulgated by norms which legitimated violence in the family (Fattah, 1979; Straus, 1976; Weis & Weis, 1975).

SPLITS IN SELF-IMAGE: TWO ILLUSTRATIONS

The splits that the victim undergoes between unconscious and conscious levels of the self provide an arena rich in reparative potential for the therapist cognizant of these issues. (See Reparation section for particulars on implementation.) In these vignettes, emphasis is placed on the relevance of taking into account both individual psychological levels as well as the larger societal views that are reflected back to the victim in assessing the vicissitudes in the victim's self-image.

Congruent Unconscious and Zeitgeist Self-Image
Split Off from Traditional Societal Level

The victim who possesses an unconscious grandiose self (Kohut, 1971) harbors the unconscious fantasy that he or she is omnipotent, invulnerable, and self-sufficient. On the conscious social level this unconscious self-image is bolstered by zeitgeist feminism that underscores the development of an autonomous, assertive self.

Prior to the victimization, this victim is thus experiencing a rare sense of well-being in feeling part of a larger social support system that serves as an appreciative mirror to heighten self-esteem. Following victimization, this strengthened self-image may then be split off from the traditional social level which culturally legitimates (Fattah, 1979) passivity and helplessness in women.

For the rape victim, the rape may now confirm the traditional view, resulting in a double narcissistic blow in that both her unconscious image of omnipotence and conscious self-sufficient image have been simultaneously assaulted by the trauma. The split-off vulnerable self that has heretofore rigorously been defended against now again surfaces to imperil the assertive aspect of self.

Congruent Unconscious and Traditional Self-Image
Split Off from Zeitgeist Level

For the masochistic victim type, the unconscious fantasies of being helpless and dependent match the traditional societal view of blaming and derogating the victim who is perceived as inept, weak, or altogether invisible—a portrait that closely resembles this victim's remembered role and internalized self-image in his or her family of origin.

Since this victim's sense of self so closely approximates the stereotypes of the traditional societal level, being a victim is viewed as a justification of this victim's self-image in which masochism prevails as a value and life-style. The split-off aspect of self for this victim is the assertive, constructive self that was given little opportunity to develop in the early years. The masochistic victim thereby exhibits particular difficulties in the area of self-reparation since the crime incident serves to further consolidate a long-standing masochistic self-image. Further, the split-off nonmasochistic self may rarely have been manifested, thereby constituting a severe developmental deficit for this victim. Lack of exposure to the zeitgeist level and/or the inability of feminist ideology to partially

Reparation

Following victimization, the victim begins the work of self-reparation. Bard and Sangrey (1979) assert "other people are the key to ultimate repair" (p. 12). While supportive others contribute to the rebuilding of self-esteem in the victim, it is equally important for the victim to focus on his or her self-image and belief system vis-à-vis the crime. Both external supports to bolster the victim's flagging self-esteem and the therapeutic integration of splits in the victim's self-image serve as major components of the reparative process.

The victim who views the victimization as a narcissistic blow to his or her fantasies of omnipotence is particularly difficult to treat, since the therapist must deal not only with a self rendered vulnerable through victimization, but must also address the victim's attempt at developing a grandiose self (Kohut, 1971) as a structure to repair the damage wrought by lack of parental appreciation at the age-appropriate period for the formation of a cohesive self and healthy narcissism.

The therapist would, in such instances, relate the current victimization to developmental self issues in an attempt to eventually link the victim's split-off grandiose self that is allegedly invulnerable to the conscious vulnerable self that is disillusioned and enraged by the victimization. It is important for the therapist to be aware of the disillusionment, and thus not initially confront such patients with the unrealistic nature of their expectations, since such interpretations are construed as criticisms and further assaults on the vulnerable self.

For masochistic and paranoid victims, reparative efforts are likewise rendered extremely difficult since the victimization constitutes an affirmation of their stance in the world. With these victims, the therapeutic task of reparation would consist of:

1. having the victim gradually come to acknowledge the splits in self;
2. examining the function that the masochistic or paranoid self serves for the victim;
3. examining the function that the now primarily split-off nonmasochistic or nonparanoid self plays in the victim's life;
4. examining the impact of the crime in the ascendancy of the masochistic or paranoid self.

At this point, the therapist can utilize one or both procedures to facilitate reparation of the damaged self:

1. The therapist may continue to closely examine the two aspects of self in terms of their meaning in the victim's life, along with their adaptive and defensive functions. In this way, the victim is gradually able to repair the splits by acknowledging their existence and working through such conflicts, so that eventually the masochistic and paranoid aspects of self diminish in intensity and the nonmasochistic and nonparanoid aspects of self can again occupy the foreground.
2. The therapist can likewise or in conjunction with the above utilize the Gestalt empty-chair technique to repair the splits in self-image. (See Perls [1969] for a description of this technique.) With this approach, over time, the victim is able to experience disavowed or partially disavowed aspects of self and, in turn, gradually effect an integration of the splits.

Other therapeutic approaches place greater emphasis on the victim's role in self-repair. Community-based self-defense programs are designed to enable the victim to regain a sense of efficacy via strengthening of the bodily self. Feminist-oriented shelters to house victims of marital abuse aid the victim in coping with a shattered self by demonstrating new possibilities for living with dignity away from the abusive spouse. This new arrangement enables the split-off hopeful self to repair self-esteem by offering alternatives to a long-endured, unbearable situation.

Many victims institute concrete behavioral strategies to regain a sense of control. Friedman et al. (1982) found that two-thirds of the New York City victims interviewed took immediate safety precautions at home, such as installing new locks or burglar alarm systems. Cohn's (1974) research on robbery victims also found that some victims institute "rational" measures, such as carrying less money to render the self less vulnerable.

Burgess and Holmstrom (1976) have focused on the cognitive and behavioral strategies that rape victims employed. The therapist and/or supportive others' acknowledgment of such coping strategies helps rebuild a sense of self-esteem in the victim. With victims who adopted different coping strategies, the therapist can either focus on what the victim was able to do to offset the severity of the crime or commend those victims who did nothing, since in so doing they were able to avoid getting hurt and stay alive.

In lieu of viewing such compliant behavior as self-destructive or regressive, the therapist can emphasize the adaptive survival value of such a stance. This emphasis on the correctness of whatever the victim did (Symonds, 1980) serves to repair the damaged self and to heighten self-esteem. Therapy can likewise include educative strategies to reduce the risk of future victimization and thus enable the victim to continue to develop a sense of personal efficacy.

CONCLUSION

The assault on the self that accompanies victimization impels crime victims to come to terms with the damaged self. The transformations undergone by the self following the crime include: lowered self-esteem, excessive employment of defenses, and/or exacerbation of self pathology.

This paper examines the phenomenon of splitting of the self-image following victimization. The therapist who is cognizant of the import of splitting on the victim's self image can help the victim acknowledge such splits in self and reparatively integrate these disowned parts into the self totality. Specific therapeutic strategies and coping skills are examined that are instrumental in the reparation of the damaged self.

The splits in the victim's self image are conceptualized as occurring on three primary levels: unconscious self images, traditional societal level, and zeitgeist level. The latter two levels represent the impact of broader social forces on the victim. The traditional societal level involves the victim's internalization of long-standing traditional values filtered through the parents. Such values often constitute the ''second injury'' (Symonds, 1980) to victims in which family, friends, and the community-at-large chastise, blame, or derogate the victim. The zeitgeist level represents ideologies-in-transition. The zeitgeist force that has exerted the profoundest influence on crime victims is feminism. Feminist-based victims' services have been involved in multiple reparative activities for victims, including teaching self-defense and providing shelters for battered women.

Two examples are provided to illustrate how the victim experiences splits between the unconscious and conscious levels of self. These vignettes elucidate the importance of both the psychological and broader social levels for the victim in both the splitting process and the gradual integration of splits to repair the self. Both therapist and victim must acknowledge the impact of all three levels on the victim's self image in order to effectively integrate disowned aspects of self into a cohesive self image.

REFERENCES

Bard, M., & Sangrey, D. (1979). *The crime victim's book.* New York: Basic Books.

Bem, S.L., & Bem, D.J. (1970). Case study of a nonconscious ideology: Training the woman to know her place. In D.J. Bem (Ed.), *Beliefs, attitudes and human affairs* (pp. 178-193). Monterey, CA: Brooks/Cole.

Bulman, R., & Wortman, D. (1977). Attribution of blame and coping in the 'real world': Severe accident victims react to their lot. *Journal of Personality and Social Psychology, 35,* 351-363.

Burgess, A., & Holmstrom, L. (1976). Coping behavior of the rape victim. *American Journal of Psychiatry, 13,* 413-417.

Cobb, S. (1976). Social support as a moderator of life stress. *Psychosomatic Medicine, 38,* 300-314.

Cohn, Y. (1974). Crisis intervention and the victim of robbery. In I. Drapkin & E. Viano (Eds.), *Victimology: A new focus* (Vol. 2). Lexington, MA: Lexington Books.

Drapkin, I., & Viano, E. (1974). *Victimology.* Lexington, MA: Lexington Books.

Fattah, E. (1979). Some recent developments in victimology. *Victimology, 4*(2), 198-213.

Freud, S. (1961). Fetishism. In J. Strachey (Ed. and Trans.) *The standard edition of the complete psychological works of Sigmund Freud.* London: Hogarth Press. (Original work published 1927).

Friedman, K., Bischoff, H., Davis, R., & Person, A. (1982, July). Samaritan blues. *Psychology Today,* pp. 26-28.

Grotstein, J. (1981). *Splitting and projective identification.* New York: Jason Aronson.

Horowitz, M. (1976). *Stress response syndromes.* New York: Jason Aronson.

Janoff-Bulman, R. (1979). Characterological versus behavioral self-blame: Inquiries into depression and rape. *Journal of Personality and Social Psychology, 37,* 1798-1809.

Kappel, S., & Leuteritz, E. (1980). Wife battering in the Federal Republic of Germany. *Victimology, 5*(2-4), 225-239.

Klein, M. (1953). *Love, hate and reparation.* London: Hogarth Press.

Kohut, H. (1971). *The analysis of the self.* New York: International University Press.

Krupnick, J. (1980). Brief psychotherapy with victims of violent crime. *Victimology, 5*(2-4), 347-354.

Kutash, I. (1978). Treating the victim of aggression. In I. Kutash, S. Kutash, & L. Schlesinger (Eds.), *Violence: Perspectives on murder and aggression.* San Francisco: Jossey-Bass.

Lerner, M., & Miller, D. (1978). Just world research and the attribution process: Looking back and ahead. *Psychological Bulletin, 85,* 1030-1051.

Lister, E. (1982). Forced silence: A neglected dimension of trauma. *American Journal of Psychiatry, 139,* 872-876.

Maracek, J., & Kravetz, D. (1977). Women and mental health: A review of feminist change efforts. *Psychiatry, 40*(4), 323-329.

Perls, F.S. (1969). *Gestalt therapy verbatim.* Lafayette, CA: Real People Press.

Perls, F.S., Hefferline, R., & Goodman, P. (1951). *Gestalt therapy: Excitement and growth in the human personality.* New York: Delta.

Reiff, P. (1979). *The invisible victim: The criminal justice system's forgotten responsibility.* New York: Basic Books.

Straus, M. (1976). Sexual inequality, cultural norms and wife-beating. *Victimology, 4*(1), 54-70.

Symonds, M. (1980, Spring). The 'second injury' to victims. *Evaluation and Change.* Special Issue.

Walker, L. (1980). Battered woman. In A. Brodsky & R. Hare-Mustin (Eds.), *Women and psychotherapy.* New York: Guilford Press.

Weis, K., & Weis, S. (1975). Victimology and the justification of rape. In I. Drapkin & E. Viano (Eds.), *Victimology: A new focus* (Vol. 3). Lexington, MA: Lexington Books.

Winnicott, D. (1965). Ego distortion in terms of the true and false self. In *The maturational processes and the facilitating environment.* London: Hogarth Press.

I Was an Incest Victim

Anonymous

On the surface, it seemed I had everything a woman could want: youth, a government job, and the love of a man I'll call Ed. He was my former writing professor, who enriched my life in many areas. He taught me to appreciate several new things, from a hike on a March day to Jewish cooking. We shared interests in music, literature, and other arts. He had rare empathy and the ability to put my needs above his.

For years, however, we didn't have sex (he compared his love for me with the love of the troubadours for their ladies, whom they loved from afar). You see, this isn't really a story about Ed and me. It's a story about incest.

When I met Ed, I had just been divorced, after 5 traumatic years. Even with all the good points of our relationship, I couldn't decide whether to make a commitment to Ed. He constantly pressed me to marry him or at least to live with him. Although he was 26 years older than I, age did not make a difference. I loved getting to know him and being in the company of such a refined, sensitive, and intellectual person. But the idea of commitment stirred conflicting emotions. I loved Ed—of that I was sure. But, deep in the recesses of my mind, I felt cold terror. It went deeper than the memory of my unhappy marriage, which I'd ended 18 months after I met Ed. My thoughts went around and around on the idea of commitment for months. Eventually I became so confused that I decided to consult a psychologist.

Gradually, with his help, I was able to recreate some scenes from my past. They are lodged in my mind as clearly as color transparencies:

—Scene one: My father is fondling me; I am 4 years old. I am so frightened that at night I arrange my stuffed animals around my bed as a defense. When I try to express my terror to my mother, she just brushes me off with, ''Don't be a baby.''

—Scene two: I am a teenager, suffering constant ''punishments'' from my father for undefined infractions. My father has bought a new family car and is taking my three brothers and

---

The author of this article is a writer for industrial publications. She prefers to remain anonymous.

© 1985 by The Haworth Press, Inc. All rights reserved.

99

100   PSYCHOTHERAPY AND THE TERRORIZED PATIENT

mother out in it for a ride, leaving me at home as "punishment." I watch through the window as the whole family except myself gets into the car and drives away.

—Scene three: My grandmother (on my mother's side) and my mother tell me outright that my father doesn't love me. They mean it as an indictment of his coldness, rather than to depress me, but I am stunned because I know in that instant that they are right.

These are not the bitter little memories which everyone harbors about their past, but a gradually surfacing pattern of treatment by my father. In therapy, I learned that my father's reactions resulted from suppressed sexual desire. He vented his frustration by being a cruel, abusive parent. Feeling the brunt of his rejection, I felt I'd done something outrageous to lose my father's love.

At one time—to be factual—he did seem to love me. One of my earliest experiences was the time he lavishly praised some of my writing, which was mostly scribbles. Right after this, the incidents of molestation began. The juxtaposition of these early experiences profoundly affected my life. The last scene of love embedded in memory was my father's praise for my writing—which, despite subsequent events, probably accounts for my determination to succeed as a writer.

Although my father dreamed of writing, he never made any attempts to write. His problems—drinking and gambling—interfered with any constructive activity. He lost every job he ever had, from warehouseman to mail sorter.

The years of my childhood and adolescence made me feel as if I was in a cage. When I was six my brother Van was born, followed by two more brothers, Kris and Terry, a few years later. My father established a close relationship with Van, which contributed toward my feeling even more displaced.

I avoided people, broke those friendships which I had allowed to develop, started quarrels and avoided group activities. Since my father had hurt me and my mother would not support me, I didn't feel I could trust anyone. Naturally, these personality traits precluded my gaining the approval of others, which intensified the feelings of rejection I'd experienced from my father.

Those feelings became particularly strong when I was 14. I completely accepted the thought of committing suicide, and sought the means to do it, but fortunately I realized I was in emotional trouble and pulled myself out by focusing on new interests: drawing and schoolwork.

About this time, my mother and I entered a terrific struggle. She resented the long hours I spent over my books and always exhorted me to be more sociable. I expressed no interest in clothes, in dating, or even in establishing friendships with other teenagers.

As I neared graduation, one teacher suggested I try to get a scholarship. However, I decided to accept my grandmother's offer to live with her and attend Duquesne University. She had accumulated a few thousand dollars from acting as nursemaid-companion for a lawyer's sick wife and promised to pay my tuition.

My grandmother lived a 20-minute streetcar ride away from the university, in Hazelwood, a milltown just oustide Pittsburgh. Grandma (my mother's mother) represented a pivotal force in my life. She had always assured my family of a steady supply of meals, clothing, and my eyeglasses when my father spent our money on binges. Her husband became an invalid when she was 21, leaving her with two children to support. She raised them alone, working the menial jobs available to a woman with a sixth-grade education. Partly as a result of her experiences, she believed women should be educated. She encouraged me to go to college. On the other hand, my mother wanted me to be a saleslady in a department store.

The next 4 years at Duquesne were the happiest of my life. I no longer had to struggle against my mother's desires that I behave a certain way, or my father's put-downs. I never realized the effect my family had on me, except through indirection. After I had lived with my grandmother 6 months, she commented on how I began smiling for the first time. I thought I had put all troubles with my family behind me. I didn't realize until I had psychotherapy that my family, particularly my father, had caused major setbacks in my social and psychological development. For one thing, the 12 years of living with my father's rejection had made me desperate for approval. I was willing to risk everything just to have someone like me.

That's where my husband Roger entered the picture. I didn't love him—he bragged incessantly and frequently rage boiled up inside me as I listened—but he was the only source of approval in my life. I felt I might never get another chance for love. My mother didn't seem to understand the turmoil I was going through. Several times, when I was on the point of giving Roger back his ring, she defended him sharply, saying I was cutting myself off from love.

Before the wedding, I was paralyzed with conflict. Roger made all the arrangements, including sending out invitations. The 2 days before the wedding I spent alone in my apartment, crying. I felt an overwhelming sadness throughout the whole period. Later, I learned in psychotherapy (although now I feel it should have been obvious) that the sexual aspects of marriage reminded me of the episodes with my father. Marriage represented my first appropriate, adult sexual experience; until then, I had never expressed an interest in sex.

Soon after I was married I realized that I had married Roger only because I felt I could not do better. A great weight seemed to be resting on my shoulders. I felt I had wrecked my life. I visited a lawyer a short time afterward to ask about divorce. Suffice it to say, that although I stayed with Roger a few years, things did not improve between us. Eventually I found a high-level government job as an editor with the government and gathered confidence to leave my husband. About this time I met Ed, which also gave me support.

Therapy benefited me enormously, but it took years. Ed waited 4 years, and then gave up and found other interests. Even with the aid of therapy, the thought of marrying him, or anyone else, for that matter, left me feeling choked. Marriage, even commitment, symbolized the loss of a self I was just discovering.

The point is this: If my previous marriage had been the only unhappy event of my life, doubtless I would be married to Ed today. But I'd never had a normal childhood or adolescence—never felt free to blossom forth with my own personality, or be free to act any way I chose. I had to grow up on guard against my father, and later, against other people. At the time of Ed's interest in me, I knew I had to open up to life, but I also knew the process couldn't be rushed.

This, then, was a significant effect of incest: I may have lost the only love of my life. While my experience with incest was milder than many other cases I've read about, it affected me profoundly, in many other areas too numerous to go into here. I share my experience in the hope that other women who have been damaged emotionally from incest will see themselves and begin to heal. Incest *can* be overcome. Women have been doing it for years.

* * *

ADDENDUM by my therapist of 15 years, Dr. Alvin S. Baraff, of Washington, D.C.

In reading this essay by one of my patients, several thoughts come to mind. Her love for Ed was based on his being a very accepting father figure. It was primarily an intellectual relationship because Ann (this is not her real name) was experiencing difficulty with intimacy at the time of the relationship, which was broken up over the idea of commitment.

Also, her father was an alcoholic. In Ann's mind, receiving praise or approval of her writing was tied to her father. She always sought writing success out of a desire to win her father's love.

She had been a clinically depressed child and adolescent. No one responded. The mother sensed something was wrong and enrolled her early in school. The mother couldn't face up to the difficulty and so sent her away to school. No one knew about Ann's suicide thoughts at age 14. She felt she couldn't tell anyone because she had tried it once, unsuccessfully. Actually, Ann left out of the article the reason she rejected suicide—a religious experience, which she could have described in detail.

In my view, her grandmother, a first-generation Polish woman, was very limited. She came off looking good in the article in comparison with the rest of the family. She was the one person Ann perceived as being on her side.

Ann was immobilized at the time of her wedding because she had an extreme fear of sex. She was unknowledgeable about it. Her husband's constant talking enraged Ann. However, her mother supported the idea that a bird in the hand was worth two in the bush. After the wedding, Ann questioned whether she could have done better.

Gradually, Ann is becoming free from shame. Her self-esteem is increasing and she is less burdened by the past.

Incest 1964:
Confusion and Terror 1984

Barbara Jo Brothers

I have a more-than-a-little disconcerting story to tell about a young woman we will call Rhonda and a theme of terror in disguise. I have realized the word "terrorized" may be a more accurate and useful working diagnosis than any other. It is the terror that works the mischief in her life and it is a malevolent force extending out to her would-be helpers in insidious, veiled ways spreading, instead of mitigating, her confusion about herself. It is the terror that demands the unrelenting internal attention that inhibits her in getting on with her life. It is help in regard to the terror that she needs.

I stepped into her life with almost mystical timing. Six months earlier I would have known no better than her previous therapist in many respects. With a kind of benevolent, if eerie, synchronicity, Rhonda appeared shortly after a series of enlightening experiences of my own, sharply focused by the reading of a journal article which has made a profound difference in what I do with Rhonda (Gelinas, 1983). I am moved to write this article to contribute toward the general clarity of this disturbing issue as manifested in Rhonda. I am afraid there are many more Rhonda's than any of us want to think about. I am also afraid that a cultural (perhaps universal) repulsion to the subject inhibits us from being able to bring it into our individual awareness sufficiently *to* think about it. I am not at all sure I would spend much time on it myself if I didn't have Rhonda to deal with several times a week.

The story: After 4 years of intense therapy involving several sessions per week and a great deal of informal contact between Rhonda and her therapist, her therapy was rather abruptly terminated by her therapist's moving out of town several hours drive away. According to Rhonda, the therapist told her that, even though therapy was terminated and she needed no further therapy, they could continue their relationship as friends; she was invited to come and visit on some weekends. On a recent such visit, Rhonda had been instructed by the previous therapist to resume

---

Barbara Jo Brothers, MSW from Tulane University in 1965, is a licensed social worker now in the full-time practice of individual and group psychotherapy.

© 1985 by The Haworth Press, Inc. All rights reserved. *105*

therapy. (The passing of the popularity of the psychoanalytic styles of therapy may have freed us to do the kind of innovative work necessary in working with schizophrenia, where involvement of the person of the therapist is not only a nice touch, but essential to the process. This work requires the kind of plunging into the confusing pool of countertransference/transference down to levels where the layers mix. What would have once been called ''acting out'' on the part of the therapist and patient is now therapeutic technique. Unfortunately, with the passing of the play-by-the-rules-only philosophy of treatment, also pass clear guidelines to distinguish unconscious, untherapeutic acting out on the part of the patient and therapist from that necessary extra extension of self. This entire termination/referral episode is the subject for another whole article which must be noted only in passing here. Aspects *are* pertinent for what we are considering here.)

Rhonda subsequently found her way to me, presenting as a delightful new patient. She is articulate, bright, introspective, and was generally pleasant as well as well groomed and attractive. A mental health professional herself, she talked about her work being very important to her and satisfying in many ways. She continued, for several sessions, to be all of those things. Then, immediately following another visit with the previous therapist which had immediately followed her decision to break up with her female lover and expand her horizons, suddenly she was unraveled and consumed with intense guilt. In retrospect, it is like an Escher painting and *now* I see symbol layered upon symbol (Hofstadter, 1980). (The breaking up with the lover was a metaphor for the breaking up with the previous therapist which was a metaphor for ''breaking up with'' her *father*.) In the first few sessions, she had described a bizarre-sounding kind of relationship between her father and herself . . . possessive and clearly symbolically incestuous even to Rhonda's perception. Being in the mental health field, she had done a considerable amount of thinking about her family's dynamics. She did not remember actual physical incest and did not believe it had actually occurred. There was, however, something in her eyes that said to *me* that it had.

Up to the point of that visit, Rhonda seemed to suffer ''merely'' from that kind of work-hard, too-much-caretaking-of-others sort of depression fairly common to mental health professionals. Up to that point, I'd had a hard time understanding how the former therapist had told her she could pick her diagnosis: schizophrenia or alcoholism. *After* the unraveling visit which was followed by another visit, I could well imagine having made the same assumptions and agreeing that much of what the therapist had done was what I would have considered many-to-most of the right things.

Yes, Rhonda reported abuse of alcohol; yes, she seemed, on occasions, to be in a fugue state or ''disoriented as to time and place.'' If I had found her lying on *my* diving board at 3:00 a.m., I might very well have thought

I was right to think of her as borderline. She shows evidence of deep unmet dependency needs, impulsive behavior, problems in intimate interpersonal relationships (but only, apparently, when sex is involved). Except for my information about the persisting negative effect of incest, when a friend of hers (who is a mental health professional with a reputation of skill and competence) called me at 1:30 a.m. and told me she thought Rhonda should be hospitalized because she was, at that moment, "disassociative and suicidal," I would certainly have thought, "Borderline," just like the previous therapist thought.

Rhonda herself thinks she is borderline. She has sufficient professional acumen to have impressed her colleagues to the extent that two different psychiatrists, friends of mine, have independently and spontaneously commented to me about her clinical skills, without any knowledge that she is in treatment with me. Rhonda looks at her own behavior and her family dynamics and concludes that her former therapist and her family must be right, she must be crazy. Rhonda's guilt level is extremely high. It is not hard to convince her that something is her fault.

I am a voice crying in the wilderness to Rhonda and to others like her, "You were a victim of incest. All your bizarre behavior can be explained as an attempt to deal with your *terror.*"

On page 315 of Gelinas' article, she points out:

> The range of symptoms and problems seen in former incest victims and described in the incest literature can be accounted for by three underlying negative effects: (1) chronic traumatic neurosis (with secondary elaborations arising from lack of treatment) (2) continuing relational imbalances (with secondary elaborations arising from lack of treatment) and (3) increased intergenerational risk of incest . . .

She goes on to say, "The intensity of the affect during this process can be disconcerting for both patient and therapist, and it can easily be mistaken as psychotic decompensation."

In Rhonda's case, she does not yet *consciously* remember the events. Recently, she has begun to have flashback memories of being in bed with her father. However, even talking *about* these memories brings up such intense pain and fear that Rhonda goes into what appears to be a trance-like state in my office. (During these states, she talks about hating her body and wanting her body to cease to exist.) She describes intense fear and it is clear to me how she could have developed amnesia for such an event as a way of dealing with the terror.

Her former therapist stated that Rhonda would refuse to discuss the possibility of an incestuous relationship with her father and would not talk about her father at all. As I listened to Rhonda's account of her relationship with this therapist, I concluded that Rhonda and the therapist had colluded to act out the original incest on a symbolic basis. I began to direct the therapy toward helping the patient step outside the system of her previous therapist/previous lover/previous lover's previous therapist to help her see the parallels between *her* acting out and her early trauma with her father. Rhonda was beginning to have shadowy, unclear kinds of memories and images and was experiencing a high level of anxiety as this material began to come into her consciousness. In the middle of this, Rhonda made one of the weekend visits to the previous therapist's home. At this point, she was tormented by the ambiguity that had existed in her family, the family's pattern of denial of reality. She had been in recent contact with her family and had experienced a recent clear example of a bizarre incident involving her father and his way of pretending like an event never happened. During the visit, according to the therapist, the patient suddenly stated, "My father started fucking me when I was 8 years old. . . ." The therapist told Rhonda this was inappropriate material to be brought up outside a therapy context. To her, this was evidence of Rhonda's psychosis. According to Rhonda, the former therapist cut her off sharply and was subsequently concerned about the effect of this statement on the therapist's own roommate (who had been the therapist of Rhonda's ex-lover). The therapist had said something like, "What do you mean bringing up a subject like that here! You don't know what *our* histories are . . ." Of course, we all know how events can become garbled as they are described to people who were not present by various people who were. Nonetheless, this therapist had made passing reference during *our* one telephone contact, to the effect that her roommate had not slept well that night. As she made this comment in the middle of a description of Rhonda's symptoms, I had to consider the possibility that the events went the way my patient said they went. Otherwise, why was her roommate's sleep pertinent to the discussion.

The former therapist described what happened in that weekend as her setting limits which the impulse-ridden patient couldn't handle . . . which was why Rhonda had left their home precipitously a day or two early. (The therapist did freely admit that she had felt more confused by this patient and experienced more countertransference in regard to her than any patient she had had during her entire career.) Rhonda described having experienced double messages and projection of her therapist's anxiety about the incest issue.

My own conclusion was that Rhonda had not been able to bring the incestuous material into consciousness during her previous therapy because of the feelings it roused in the therapist. (A person needs to feel a certain amount of safety and security in order to be able to bring up such a terrifying subject. Unconscious resistance on the part of the therapist would translate as lack of sufficient support.) It seemed to me that much of

Rhonda's acting-out behavior could be accounted for by the fact that the material had remained unconscious, as described in Gelinas' article.

Rhonda does not seem to quite fit the borderline picture. At this point, I am not sure whether the psychotic-appearing behavior is an attempt to deal with the terror of the traumatic event or whether she is, in fact, a borderline personality who *also* suffered sexual abuse from her father. Considering the damage to her self-esteem from her family's having told her she was crazy, from her father's pattern of extreme denial, and her former therapist's behavior serving as a reenactment of the family experience, I have hesitated to suggest psychological testing because I believe the main issue is repressed trauma. She calls herself crazy as a way of getting her father off the hook which results in her turning the rage against herself and subsequently results in self-destructive behavior.

As long as she attempts to protect her father (who was the parent from whom she received the bulk of her nurturing) she has to consider herself "the one to blame." The self-blame, guilt response in the case of sexual abuse is pervasive. In a very different sort of child abuse case, the 18-month-old son of another one of my patients was molested by his 13-year-old female babysitter. The child, now three, kept this event in his mind until he had learned to talk well enough to describe it to his mother. During his recounting of what had happened, he said, "Mama, I didn't try to stop her." His mother told him nobody expects an 18-month-old child to be able to fight off anybody in any sort of attack. With that kind of maternal reassurance, the little boy won't have to grow up thinking he had somehow brought that all on himself as he might otherwise be very likely to do, ludicrous as it sounds to the listener. Rhonda's case is much more complicated. The aggressor and the person with the role of protector/nurturer are the same person. This puts Rhonda in a terrible double-bind: If she admits he betrayed her in such a profound way, she must question what she has learned of what love is all about; if she does *not* admit the betrayal, she convicts herself as crazy to be plunged into such depths of despair and depression by a fantasy she must be making up.

At this point, when even a reference is made to her father, Rhonda begins to weep and goes into a disassociative state within seconds of the material coming up. Gelinas' point is very clear to me when I watch Rhonda enter that internal state of terror, which I believe is the result of an event that was too terrifying for her to remember intellectually but which she carries with her nonetheless, in her body/feeling memory and in her behavioral patterns. Rhonda is trying to deal with a severely traumatic event or repeated events by "re-living" it without consciously acknowledging what it is, in much the same way that such phenomena occurs in war veterans who were involved in traumatic, violent events.

I, too, find it anxiety provoking to witness her pain and search for the truth of her responses around this issue. Rhonda is such a warm, pleasant,

PSYCHOTHERAPY AND THE TERRORIZED PATIENT

alert person when she is not in the disassociative state that I find myself tempted to want to "keep" her there by making no references to her father. A case could be made for teaching her more facile access to her adult ego state (as described by Eric Berne's (1966) transactional analysis . . . parent, adult, child ego states). There is a big difference, however, between teaching her to bring herself out of what appear to be altered states of consciousness and between the kind of "putting in an ego" that one does in the case of the schizophrenic. The necessity of doing the latter is a conclusion to which one might easily come if that person did not have the information about the symptoms, if you will, that indicate the presence of incest in the patient's history.

I do not think there is enough awareness in the therapeutic community about the *nature* of the negative effects, in adult victims, of incest during childhood. It is terror, insufficiently and inadequately addressed.

REFERENCES

Gelinas, D. J. (1983). The persisting negative effects of incest. *Psychiatry. 16.*312-332.
Hofstadter, D. R. (1980). *Godel, Escher, Bach: An eternal golden braid.* New York: Vintage Books.
Berne, E. (1966). *Principles of group treatment.* New York: Oxford University Press.

Entitlement:
A Meditation for the Psychotherapy Patient
(To be read aloud to oneself)

Joseph C. Zinker

ENTITLE: "`. . .` to give a right or claim to `. . .` to empower" *Winston Dictionary;* "`. . .` to name, to designate" *Merriam/Webster Dictionary;* "Someone must come along sometime in our lives and tell us, as a witness to a great event might do, 'Yes, yes, you are here and yes, you are entitled to be here fully `. . .`' " *Anonymous.*

INTRODUCTION

This little article started as an effort to make a "prayer" or meditation for several of my patients—a kind of homework to be read once or twice a month. I wanted to create a vehicle the use of which would remind them of their entitlements, rights, and privileges that they seem to forget or remain blinded to in spite of months and months of psychotherapy efforts.

I. THE WORLD AND MY BELOVED

If I am lucky, I have at least one person in the world who cares about me. This person can be my parent, a child, spouse, teacher, student, friend, companion, work partner, neighbor, or my therapist. This person need not be my lover but I think of him or her as my "beloved."

I deserve to be loved by someone who is important to me, whom I respect and value. I deserve to be cared about.

My beloved is here for me. My beloved is not just a person, but a message, a metaphor of the world. My beloved *is* the world. What I see in him or her, I can also see in the forest, in flowers, in animals, in all the people, in friends. My beloved opens my eyes and helps me see the world.

Because of this experience, I know that I deserve to see, feel, and ex-

---

Joseph C. Zinker received his PhD in clinical psychology from Western Reserve University in 1963. He is the founder of the Cleveland Gestalt Therapy Institute and a member of the professional staff. Dr. Zinker maintains a private practice of psychotherapy.

© 1985 by The Haworth Press, Inc. All rights reserved. *111*

press myself in relation to the world in the same way that I see and feel with her or him. My friend takes my hand and takes me into the world. I can see its fullness, its beauty, its dangers, its cruelty, its ugliness, because I can see these things in her or him.

My beloved takes my hand, saying, "This is your world, see and do with it what you see and do with me." My beloved has a crystal-clear message for me: "You are whole, good, kind, strong, imaginative, and you are a world citizen . . . you belong here . . . this is yours, this is your world. . . ."

II. NATURE

I have a responsibility to nature because I have a relationship with it. Nature deserves my care, my protection, and my respect. And nature is there for me. The sky and the moon and the earth and the trees and the flowers and the waters are there for me.

I deserve to fully enjoy everything living (and not living) around me. I can put my feet into the cool pond and I can let the sun shine on my face because I deserve to enjoy these phenomena—I am nature. Nature and I are one (just as my beloved and I are one). Therefore, it is perfectly natural for me to travel, to fly, to swim, to hike, to walk and run, to pick flowers, to play in the rain, to speak to everything that interests me and heightens my energy.

I am on good terms with nature—my own nature and nature of the world outside me. I please nature when I live a full, happy life; and nature is there to support me. The streets and houses are there for me, the shaded alleys are there for me, the wind and snow are there for me, the puddles and animals are there for me, the crickets and birds are there for me, all the pretty and ordinary sounds are there for me (and I am allowed to make pretty and ordinary sounds with pleasure). Even the vacant lots are mine, the roads and bridges are mine, the canals and pleasure boats are mine, the banks and police are mine—they are there to take care of me, to lubricate the freedom of movement I have in the world.

I deserve to enjoy nature. I am nature. I deserve to express my nature out there in the world.

III. PEOPLE

I am one of millions. But I am as no one else is. I am unique. Like any other person in this world, I am here part-time. And during this time I will show respect to those who show me their respect—and I will avoid people who are disrespectful and poisonous to me. Because I deserve to be happy among people, I like pleasing and taking care of others and I deserve to be pleased and taken care of by others. Just as I am there for (and with) others, they, in turn, are there for me.

People "belong" to me and I to them, in the sense that we all share this world equally. I am not bigger than others, nor are they bigger than I am. I deserve to be loved and cherished, to be seen, to be appreciated, to be praised, to be touched, to be hugged and kissed. People are mine. People are good for me (mostly). They give me what I ask for and want. They will attend to me because I show my right to be attended to. I deserve to be shown respect. I deserve to be given work, food, money, because I am a contributor to people and to the world.

People walk in the streets. It is sunny. And they are beautiful. They are pleased to see me and they smile at me. Women smile and say hello, with pleasure, to me. Children love me and men greet me with pleasure. People behold me with pleasure. I can ask for anything from people because I am lovely and good and kind, and I deserve to partake of their generosity and love. I deserve to do anything I please. I belong here. I belong with people. I can go anywhere and do anything I please, as long as I am not mean or destructive to others. I belong to the social fabric of this world and I am happy being among people. People will often go out of their way to please me. Why? Because I am me and I deserve to be pleased . . . and because I repeatedly please others.

IV. WORK

I deserve to do the work that turns me on! I am a worker. I love my work. How do I know that my work is not just my "job?" Because my work and I are friends. Because my work stimulates my curiosity and my energy. Because I work with people. My work and I are one, just as my beloved and I are one. I don't separate "work" from "pleasure." My work is one form of pleasure because I express all of me in my work. My work is one of my thrusts in life. It gives me direction. I organize much of my life around my work. Work is growth for me!

As I grow, mature, learn, read, go to the movies, travel—as I do all these things—my work gets better and richer and more skillful and elegant. I give my heart and soul to my work, and people are pleased with what I create. My presence enhances people and helps them become more of who they are. My presence makes people feel affirmed, whole, good, "right" on the inside. And their presence affirms me.

Employers are pleased to pay me for my work. It is only one limited way they can show their gratitude for my giving. I deserve to be paid, to have all the money I need to take care of myself and my family. I deserve to earn a good living.

114   PSYCHOTHERAPY AND THE TERRORIZED PATIENT

I deserve to use my money any way I please: to take care of my house, to travel, to buy presents for myself and others. I deserve to live well and fully. I have earned this right with my struggling, my reading, my experiences, my education, and my work. I need not falsely humble my accomplishments to others. I need not render myself smaller than I am or bigger than I really feel to gain the respect of others. I simply need to show myself, to make myself visible.

As a worker, a friend, a member of a group or family, as a person who makes myself known and seen in the world, I deserve to live my life fully, with pleasure, and to pass the pleasure on to others.

V. RELATIVES

Oh, relatives, they are so problematical. They—our mothers and fathers—created us and loved us the best way they knew how. Parents can't please us. Parents, brothers, sisters, and cousins are human beings! They are not fully qualified (nor should they be) to "make us happy" and to fulfill all our needs. They can't. Sometimes parents—mostly out of their own hunger and bitterness—can hurt us deeply. Sometimes parents can damage us irreparably. An no one can give us back our early purity and innocence. No one can fully re-parent us. But we long to go back to our parents, our roots, over and over again to be loved and affirmed, to be praised and to be held—to be told we are "good," we are "gifted," and we are "special."

I must learn to take the best of my parents and to spit out the parts that don't fit or that hurt me. I must learn to have boundaries and to have my own identity and not to depend on my parents to affirm me.

Relatives are people. Some people can give and others just want to take, to sap us of our good nature, of our vitality. Some people get pleasure from praising us, while others prefer to "make" us feel obligated and to "make" us feel guilty. So is the world. And the world of our parents is the same world. But we don't have to swallow what others give us.

We must learn to be separate—to affirm our own goodness and wholeness. I deserve to be loved, and if my parents or my family can't give me affirmation, I can move into the vast world of people and help myself to what is there for me, what is possible, what is offered.

For the most part, the world of people is good. People have pleasure giving and when I take from them (that which didn't come from family), I give others satisfaction. The more people give to me, the more generous I feel toward them. It is in this repeated bridging of give and take that trust, respect, and caring become real to me.

I will be compassionate toward my parents. In loving myself fully, I will learn to forgive my parents for hurting me. In forgiving them, I will indirectly demonstrate that, in spite of their faults, they created a sweet, kind, good child: a whole human being. My parents succeeded after all. They helped create a person who is capable of compassion and forgiving—a person who is whole, a person who feels fully embedded in the world, a person who can give to others, and a person who can take the gifts of others and savor them.

I deserve to have a sense of resolution and peace about my parents. I deserve to move on—and in my own generation, to struggle with the dilemmas of doing a fine job, caring for, parenting, and mentoring others.

VI. ON BEING A VICTIM

Because I have experienced so few breaks in my life, I feel like a victim. I feel as if the world won't cooperate in my struggle to become myself. I often feel mired in the goo of daily difficulties—as if people and circumstances are dragging me down. I feel victimized.

But as I live on and grow and begin to see the light of day in psychotherapy, the very label of victim becomes an encumbrance to me. I am tempted to blame others for my own lack of energy and inner push. Self-righteously, I focus on the faults of others. When well-meaning friends try to help me and don't hit the mark, I am tempted to feel victorious over their "incompetence": No one can do "right" for me. I render my friends and family (and, at times, my therapist) helpless when I tell them that they don't understand and have never lived the sort of pain I have experienced. My pain is a badge that keeps me isolated from loved ones, keeps me feeling special in my suffering.

"If only" has become part of my daily language: "If only my parents had sent me to college," "If only I weren't maligned by my boss," "If only I had more professional opportunities," "If only I was part of the 'inner circle' in my company," "If only I could stop smoking and lose a little weight". . . ad infinitum.

I now realize that, over the years, my "If onlys" started as expressions of regret and were slowly raised to the status of shields of protection and slogans of protest against a cruel world. I have run out of regrets. Now I want to live the life which *is* possible for me, to find what is good enough for me and to live it with some pleasure.

I must learn to shed my badge of pain because I have worn it too long and it no longer serves to protect me as it did many years ago. I am entitled to find the goodness that my pain has served so I can let go of it and move on in my life. I am entitled to take back the power I have projected onto others so that I can use it directly to get what I need and want from the world.

To give up feeling the victim, I may have to live through a period of owning how I can victimize others by rendering them helpless and stupid. Only when I can recognize the aesthetically unpleasant notion of my capacity as a *victimizer,* will I learn how to carry my power fully, competently, compassionately. Unlike my elders who abused me, I will use my power to engage, to take care of, to love, to teach, and to be intimate—rather than to beat, oppress, and intimidate others. I am entitled to give up my badge of victim and to carry my strength gracefully. I am entitled to walk straight in the streets and to see the world as a place I can influence.

* * *

In caring for my friends, I am able to see the world, to see it in its wholeness, and to be a whole person. In being able to love one person, I can see the lovable parts of all others. I deserve to enjoy life, to participate in and savor nature and people. I deserve to do the work I love and to feel fully involved in my work. I deserve to work as much or as little as I please and to be well rewarded for my efforts. I deserve to be well paid for my work and to use my money in the service of living a full, rich, generous life.

I am glad to have been born, to be alive, and to strive and hope for a better life (for myself, my family, my friends). I have the right to be angry for not having received everything I needed from my parents, but that does not entitle me to hurt others. As I grow and find ways of fulfilling my needs and as my boundaries grow clearer and stronger, I will feel more compassion for others and be able to forgive them. I will strive to see all sides of people's actions, to recognize and struggle with the good and the bad in the world.